I AM JOSEPH,
YOUR BROTHER

OTHER BOOKS BY JOSEPH JERRY LEVESQUE

The 7th, To Bury the Dead
(1963) Out of print

Monk to Bootlegger:
Stories of a Wandering Canadian American
(2014) Amazon

I AM JOSEPH, YOUR BROTHER

JOSEPH JERRY LEVESQUE

ISBN-13: 978-1508552208
ISBN-10: 1508552207
Library of Congress Control Number: 2015908740

DEDICATION

To all the former Brothers of St. Joseph
who worked so hard to establish
Resurrection Cemetery

CONTENTS

THE MAVERICK MONK

Joseph draws us into his life with stories, each as unique as the religious brother, undercover bootlegger, or childhood friend whose slice of life he describes.

Joe's knowledge of the comings and goings of the earthly Kingdom of God in the form of the Catholic Church approaches encyclopedic irreverence. Joe speaks his mind, with no equivocation. Refreshing, anyone?

Each of Joseph's daily treks represents an important mission. He totes his bewildered but tolerant friends along with him as he explores the philosophy of the owner of the ethnic restaurant whose cuisine he is sampling that week. A familiar face at the do-it-yourself print shop, Joe stops in to update the graphic on his business card, mail out a copy of his book, or laminate photos of his friends into placemats.

Back at his home base, he coos sympathetically over the phone with the doting widows of his lifelong friends from other states, yet Joe is not above lambasting as Luddite his old codger friends he feels are not keeping up with technology.

Everyone from Walmart greeters to Archbishops takes note of the purposeful energy broadcast by this man, supposedly in his rocking chair years.

Some people have a paper route. Joseph has a people route that changes a little every day. If you have come this far, you may consider yourself on his route.

Maggie Abel

PREFACE

I Am Joseph, Your Brother is a sequel to my previous book, *Monk to Bootlegger: Stories of a Wandering Canadian American.* Both are an overture to the humanity of man.

Man inhabits all four corners of the earth—different colors, different languages, different cultures. We are born, we learn about what is around us, we form families, raise children, grow old, and die. The cycle repeats itself forever and ever. We die as we came in: completely naked. We are all equal, as Brothers and Sisters.

Let's hope you enjoy this eye-opener into our humanity.

ACKNOWLEDGMENTS

Many of the stories in this book were scheduled for the first book, *Monk to Bootlegger.* Limitations of the trade forced me to hold them back. So this sequel went rather fast. I then wrote more stories for this book, and must give credit to those who deserve it.

First of all, I must take my hat off to my Alter Ego, who again deserves all the credit: Maggie Abel—without whom the book would never have been written. To Dan Noreen and his wife, the poet Mary Rooney—my good friends with whom I have traveled all over Gascony—for their encouragement and suggestions on various essays. To Rachid Ayare, who was kind enough to go over my two Muslim stories to make sure they were accurate.

Last, to God/Allah, for giving me the grace and knowledge to write what I have written.

CHAPTER 1

EARLY ON

101

MY NUN

She was thirty-five, a Catholic nun, and the superior of her community. It's not that I was just eighteen and had never kissed in passion before—quite the opposite: I was thirty-three, a Catholic monk and the superior of my community! Although the two institutions were side by side, it never dawned on me to look for that famous tunnel that supposedly ran between her convent and my monastery.

Our relationship was always professional, right and proper. I found her beautiful…but what else can I say when all I could see was her face? Her religious habit covered all her body — ah! The early Fathers were right, the habit covers a multitude of sins. Nevertheless, I could not see her shape.

She was a good superior, good to the children under her care, but firm with her nuns. We were happy and admiring neighbors for one year. Then she and her community were called back to the Mother House in Wichita. My community and I were sad to see them leave; absence makes the heart grow fonder: that's how we all felt as the months flew by.

Two years later, I received a phone call from My Nun. "Brother Joseph, I have been telling the nuns here about you and your apostolate, and my sisters would love to hear more, so we decided to invite you for lunch next Sunday at noon sharp."

"It's a lovely idea! May I bring something, perhaps a bottle of red wine?"

"Absolutely not, Brother Joseph! You know we do not imbibe!"

I rolled my eyes. (I know different. They must keep up the appearances.)

At 11:30 that Sunday, Brother Joseph was ringing the doorbell at the sisters' convent. My Nun opened the door and with gravitas said, "I knew to expect you somewhat early. Won't you come in?"

It turned out the small group of nuns who wanted to see and hear me were all members of the nuns' council — the leaders of that community.

"Very well," I said, "let's eat." But first, every member of the council was introduced to me individually—most of them elderly—but I was happy to smile. A smile encourages a return smile.

I was seated at the head of the table, My Nun to my left, and Mother Superior to my right. They provided me with a wonderful Sunday lunch-dinner as only nuns can do…and the conversation was heavenly, talking about God, the angels, The Brothers of St. Joseph, and the Sisters of St. Joseph.

After a two-hour lunch, we all said grace and parted. I followed My Nun out into the Garden of Eden. Don't forget, she still wore her full nun's habit, so I could not see the multitude of sins it covered. Our walk started in a nonchalant way as long as we were in sight of the windows where all the nuns in the convent were peering from behind the blinds. My Nun guided me deeper into the garden out of sight of the peeping nuns, then relaxed and put me at ease. She grabbed my hand as we continued walking. Soon we were walking arm in arm, and the conversation was getting very personal about her dreams for happiness, and it was not about being a nun, it was about love, and more love!

I nodded in lovely assent and said, "I feel exactly the same way. And every time I do, I remind myself of my religious vow of chastity." It didn't faze her and she never skipped a beat.

My Nun placed her right arm around my waist and guided me to sit on a little stone wall. Sitting by my side, with her arm around my waist, she rested her head on my shoulder.

"Oh, Joseph, life in the convent is so hard—I think I shall die if I stay here!"

I had no sooner removed her arm from around my waist, than she placed it around my shoulders and brought her beautiful and perfect lips to mine. It was an ecstatic moment for me, melting my heart, my soul, and my entire being. I could have married her, right then and there, and no doubt, we could have consummated it that very day.

THUNDERCLAP!..........................

I knew full well she had taken her vow of chastity, yet she never spoke up when I mentioned that my precept of chastity was keeping me in check. She was putting the make on me. It turned me off.

As soon as possible I returned to my car.

"Au revoir, Sister Martinette," I said before I putted off. My rearview mirror framed the everlasting picture of Martinette crying into a white handkerchief, waving it as I drove off into the sunset.

Now that I am old and decrepit, retired and good for nothing, all I can do is cry in my beer. PS. My beer is always a Trappist dark beer.

102

JEANNINE

This is Jeannine at fifteen—when our passions were at their height. This is how I remember her, and I shall cherish this vision to the end of my life. Later I learned she had married Paul, a school friend of mine, and they had seven children.

In 2014, when I was eighty-seven, we made contact again, and I decided to vacation in Maine to visit her. I prepared us for this visit by calling her every week for two months. She gave me the names of all her children, and some of their phone numbers.

Denis	Lucie
Roger	Richard
Roland	Rachel
Paul	

Lucie and Denis

DENIS

Denis was the firstborn of the seven children, and Jeannine raised him religiously. He attended St. Peter's school in Lewiston, taught by the Brothers of the Sacred Heart. In the eighth grade, he began pestering Jeannine, telling her he felt God calling him to be a teaching Religious Brother. Jeannine felt he was too young, but relented at last.

At fourteen, Denis entered the Brothers of the Sacred Heart in Rhode Island, where he taught school for forty years, until medical problems forced him to retire. Of course, he returned to Lewiston in his retirement.

Meeting him for the first time in 2014, I was impressed by his mien and his language, similar to that of my teachers in 1943 and 1944. After I had known him for a week, it was clear he had the same fervor as Postulant Brothers, which put me to shame, even though I had been founder of a hard-working religious community. I secretly wished I was in his shoes.

One Sunday, we decided to take a drive through Maine, New Hampshire, and Vermont to see the beautiful autumn foliage. We both admired God's creation, sparkling gems of foliage covering the mountains and fields. Denis's conversation was measured and religious, remonstrating with me all day about my life away from the Catholic Church. We had a very meaningful dialog, and I enjoyed the day immensely. Denis's remonstrations were clear and apropos, and I accepted them without a word, put them in my pipe, and smoked them.

LUCIE

I decided to call Lucie and make her acquaintance. We hit it off on the first sentence. She was so easy to talk to, it seemed she was my own daughter. We joked, and we laughed.

After that, I constantly thought of Lucie. A week after my first call, I called her again. Same time, same station. The bonhomie was the same as the first time, and we were both happy to talk to each other. Then Lucie said, "You know, Jerry, you could have been my father!" She was spot on, and I replied, "Yes, Lucie, then you would have been my second sperm child!"

Her brothers call her "Loose Lips." Is it a positive or negative sobriquet? Damned if I know. I guess it depends on the circumstance. Only this week, I read that several Cardinals (no names) had called Pope Francis "Loose Lips" and in this case it was definitely negative.

PAUL

Paul is Jeanine's seventh and last child—the bottom of the pot. But you certainly don't have to scrape the pot. He is a self-made man—unusual when you have six older siblings. He is now director of all services for a large hospital in Maine. I met him on my trip to Maine in 2014, and he was so glad to meet his mother's former boyfriend that he took us out to a nice Italian restaurant. Over dinner, Paul told me the following story:

"My wife Wendy was cooking breakfast with the sliding door to the deck wide open. I was in the bedroom changing after a shower and could smell the scent of bacon throughout the house. Apparently so could a bear."

"All of a sudden I could hear Wendy yelling to come quick. I finished putting on my pants and ran into the kitchen."

Black bear

"I then saw a black bear leaving the deck and heading out around the above-ground pool.

"Wendy was out on the deck when she first saw the bear, which was attempting to get to the hanging bird feeder. The only thing between her and the bear was the screen door to the deck. She yelled to me to scare the bear off.

"The curious thing is that although the dogs were sitting near the door, they remained facing the kitchen counter. In their anticipation of their feeding, they never really looked out on the deck. I wonder what would have happened if they had seen the bear."

• • •

I was born in 1927 on the fourth floor in the back (circled). Seven years later, Jeannine was born on the second floor in front (circled). It was during the Great Depression, and her father, Sylvio, was out of work. There was no Social Security in those days. Sometimes there was a soup kitchen truck on the street, but there was not enough food to sustain them.

Sylvio had to cut expenses, so he moved his family to Knox Street.

At that time, I was seven years old and knew a baby had been born on the second floor front, but I grew up without knowing the baby's name. At that time, my family consisted of a father, a mother, and two children. So my family moved down to the second floor front. The rent on the fourth floor had been $4.00 a week, while our new second floor front apartment was $7.00 a week.

This floor was the most desirable among all the apartments in this building. The Levesques were now the 'Nouveau Riches.'

I did not meet Jeannine until 1948, when I was walking with friends in the city park one Sunday night. The rest is history (see my previous book, *Monk to Bootlegger*). At the time, Jeannine was fourteen, and I was twenty-one. I've always loved them young and tender.

In that first book, I wrote there was only two years difference in our ages. That's on account of my dementia. (You could call it "convenient dementia.") So this book will set the record straight.

Jeannine asked a friend to take this picture of us, and as soon as she had the roll developed, she presented me this signed photo. Her grown children told me they recognize the handwriting at the top as their mother's.

• • •

In October 2014, after I had already became old and gray, I flew to Lewiston, Maine, to visit Jeannine. Although she had had two major surgeries in the previous year or so, she was doing well. We were able to see each other at least four times that month. One evening we went out for dinner. I asked to take her out to the old River Road for old times' sake, but she declined. Then I told her the real reason I came back—I came to propose, the proposal I have cried for all my adult life. She cocked her head and looked at me seriously. She said, "I might be amenable—what exactly are you thinking?"

While her husband Paul was still alive and I could only pine for her, I had taken refuge in God, my Maker, in the form of a dedicated monk, building the best managed cemetery in Oklahoma, and the most unique cemetery chapel in all North America.

But now those days were behind, and now all the choices lay open before me—before us. My fully formed thoughts came tumbling out.

"Since we are both Catholic, we should ask a priest to marry us," I said. "Neither of us belongs to a parish now in Lewiston, so we must think of a wedding venue. I already have my crypt in Oklahoma, purchased pre-need, and you told me you would be buried next to Paul in St. Peter's Cemetery in Lewiston. I want to be true to you—I would want our wedding to be both symbolic and meaningful. Your father and mother are both buried in St. Peter's Cemetery, as your grandparents were; and my father, mother, and grandparents are also in St. Peter's Cemetery. So we both belong there! Why don't we find a priest who will marry us in St. Peter's Cemetery?"

Jeannine was just staring at me.

Until she broke my heart.

"Jerry, you are absolutely crazy." I was crushed! Through my despair, I wondered, could she be getting even with me for what happened sixty years ago? How could I blame her? But I'd be damned before I'd show my real emotions.

• • •

There was nothing for me to do, but return to Oklahoma. My plane was to take off from the Jetport in Portland. I drove immediately to Portland, took a motel for the night, and took off in the morning.

I arrived in Oklahoma City in late afternoon, and Duke, a friend, picked me up for the fifteen-mile trip to my house. He dropped me in front of my house, I thanked him, and off he went. As I was unlocking my door, I could hear the phone inside ringing. It was Jeannine's first-born, Denis—informing me that as I was climbing into the wild blue yonder that morning, his mother had passed away.

On the plane, I was planning on returning to Lewiston the following year, and make another attempt at proposing. Now, c'est tout fini!

I sobbed all night. Any hopes were gone.

PLEASE GOD, MAY JEANNINE REST IN PEACE!
AMEN.

FRANCO-AMERICAN

Many long-time Francofone families from France and former French protectorates from all over the world, especially French-Canada, have immigrated and settled in the United States. New England probably has the highest number of such immigrants, and Louisiana the second.

In many such families, the French language was taught and passed on to the next generation, and more generations down the line. Through the years, this language deteriorates as more and more anglicized words creep in—and sometimes you get Franglish. Depending upon the environment and language support system, sooner or later the day arrives when the lingo is unrecognizable, and the person is now an English-speaking person.

It is estimated that nearly twelve million U.S. residents are of French descent and about two million speak French at home. An additional 450,000 U.S. residents speak a French-based Creole language. In the northeast United States, Franco-American groups tend to identify more strongly with "New World" regional identity—such as French-Canadian. Louisiana identifies with the Acadians, Cajun, or Louisiana Creole. Such bonding inhibits the development of a wider French-American identity.

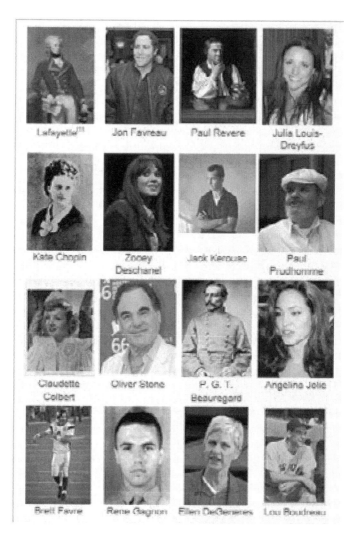

The above are all French Americans.

Anthony Bourdain   *Emeril Lagasse*
Both Bourdain and Lagasse are also French Americans.

Anthony Bourdain's family immigrated to the United States in the early 1900s from southwest France, close to Biaritz. When their son, Anthony, was born they spoke only English to him, so he knows nothing of "Le Pays Basque" of France except what he learned in school growing up.

Emeril Lagasse was born in Fall River, Massachusetts, where he was raised by his French-Canadian father and his Portuguese mother. After graduating from culinary school, he traveled to France to polish his skills. When he returned to the U.S., he spent a few years working in fine restaurants in the northeast. In 1982 he replaced Paul Prudhomme as executive chef of famed New Orleans restaurant Commander's Palace. In 1992, Emeril's was named the best new restaurant of the year by *Esquire* magazine.

104

CAJUN

French explorer Robert Cavelier de La Salle named the region Louisiana in 1682 in honor of France's Louis XIV. For forty years, I had two lady friends in Oklahoma City who were direct descendants of de La Salle—in fact, their maiden names were de La Salle. Never did I hear a French word emanating from them, and they always represented themselves as Louisiana Cajuns. Both Rita and Lena always told me that de La Salle discovered the Mississippi River, but history books confirm that it was discovered by Hernando de Soto a hundred years before de La Salle. Can't tell that to those ladies if you wish to stay alive!

Natchitoches was established in 1714 by Louis Juchereau in present-day northwest Louisiana. This French settlement was the northern terminus for the El Camino Real, and soon became a flourishing river port for sugarcane plantations. New Orleans, the headquarters of the French Administration in Louisiana, was founded in 1718. Both Rita and Lena were white, with rather dark skin. Obviously, there was some dark creole blood in their gene pool. For the sake of this story, we are going to write about the Cajuns in Louisiana.

Lower Louisiana was settled by French Colonists expelled from Acadie in Eastern Canada, who became known as Cajuns. The deportation of the Acadians is referred to as Le Grand Dérangement (The Great Upheaval).

In Louisiana, where I lived for a while, I studied the Cajun language by simply listening—call it hands-on experience—and I concluded it's a tower of babel. It seems there are various words in usage in most families, be it white, black, creole, mulato, etc. In the long run, the individual is speaking a dialect or patois, and again, it is passed on. *Plus que ça change, plus c'est la même chose.* Where it will stop, nobody knows.

Joseph Broussard led the first group of 200 Acadiens to arrive in Louisiana in 1765 aboard the Santo Domingo, which landed close to St. Martinsville.

Joseph Broussard

France ceded Louisiana to Spain in 1762, so Broussard and his cohorts landed in a benevolent Spanish possession. They were allowed to continue to speak their language, and practice their religion, which was the same as that of the Spaniards, and pursued their livelihoods with minimal interference. Through time, the Frenchmen or Cajuns who ventured to other States lost their language and identity, so only the people in Louisiana are known as Cajuns. Today, some people identify themselves as Cajun culturally despite lacking Acadian ancestry.

CREOLES

Louisiana creole people are descended from the colonial settlers in Louisiana. The term creole was used on slave inventories to distinguish locally born American slaves from those born in Africa. The most precise definition of a creole is a person of non-American ancestry, either African or European, who was born in the Americas. Some creole people have African and sometimes Native American ancestry, such as Choctaw, Natchez, and others. Creoles are a mixture of nationalities and languages, as long as the person was born in the Americas. The creole language varies from one town to another, but sometimes you can identify a person by certain words used. If you understand this jargon, you're a better writer than I am.

CAJUN LANGUAGE

Lost in the diaspora of negritude, added to bayou creole alligator lingo, is Louisiana creole. This combination of colonial and Louisiana French, and Choctaw patois and dialect—mixed with very old French nautical language and jargon ranging from St. Malo to LaRochelle and Brouage on the coast of France—makes up the Cajun language. It is nothing but intelligible, yet still Franco-American.

Example: "He goin navigate t'nite."

("He's going out on the town tonight.")

He may navigate wherever he wants to go, and he's not talking about navigating on the water.

In some small enclaves within a city or town, a few families still speak a passable French, but they are rare.

For a stranger coming to Louisiana expecting to overhear Cajun language, or expecting to converse in the supposed Cajun language, I would say, "Forget it!" It is so contorted, even in family—some members asking another family member, "What did you say?" or "What do you mean?" And let's not forget the Spanish rule with their own corrupted colonial lingo which lasted forty years. Alligator hunters on the bayou have their own creole Choctaw dialect, and other occupations have their own dialect—it goes on. They all love to coin new words.

EVANGELINE

Sculpture of Evangeline, Grand-Pre National Historic Site, Nova Scotia

Louisiana has played a great part in the history of the United States, and Cajuns have a similar place in Louisiana's past. To understand the Cajuns, one must read Evangeline, by the great American poet Henry Wadsworth Longfellow, written in English and published in 1847. He was introduced to the true story of the Acadians by another great poet, Nathaniel Hawthorne. Both of them had attended Bowdoin College in Maine. My sister Rita and niece

Brenda lived only a few houses from the college in Brunswick at one time in the 1900s. Now Brenda lives in Bowdoin, Maine (see the original *Monk to Bootlegger*).

Evangeline is written as a poem in dactylic hexameter, a poetic rhythm which is today considered archaic. It describes the betrothal of a fictional Acadian girl, Evangeline, to her beloved Gabriel and their separation as the British deport the Acadians from Acadie to Louisiana. The word Acadie was taken from the Indian word "aquoddie," the Indian name for pollack, a fish.

The poem was impactful in defining Acadian history. Longfellow presents Acadia as a utopia and Acadians as passive, peaceful, innocent people. The Acadians of Canada came mostly from northwest France. You will find many Levesques in Canada, and some in Louisiana.

The poem also led generations of protestants to sympathize with a people who were often demonized and persecuted for being Catholic.

In 1920, at Grand-Pre, Nova Scotia, Acadians reconstructed the French church with a statue of Evangeline in the courtyard.

Evangeline Memorial Cross

LEWISTON SUN & JOURNAL

1939

At the age of twelve, I applied for a paper route with the *Lewiston Daily Sun & Journal*. A month later, I was the Daily Sun paper boy on Maple Street. Summer or winter, at 4:30 each morning, I picked up my newspapers on the corner of Lisbon and Maple. Some of these houses were three or four stories high and I had to climb the stairs in pitch darkness. Having been raised in a four-story tenement house, I did not fear this trek

One morning while making my pre-dawn ascent, I sensed I tripped over a "corpse" in the second flight of stairs. This scared the hell out of me and I ran downstairs to the street, where I saw the milkman on his rounds. When I told him of my fears, he said, "Okay, son, let's go see." He pointed his flashlight at the "corpse" and turned him over.

"He's just a dead drunk tenant who won't wake up."

I ran into quite a few such situations in the following two years as a newsboy. By then, I always carried a small flashlight in my pocket and "dead-drunk corpses" never scared me again.

It was already World War II when I was a grown-up boy of fourteen, so I went to work at Lepage's Bakery after school and on weekends, on the bread slicing machine and oftentimes the ovens. The owner was Regis Lepage, who had gone to school with my dad twenty years earlier. Later on, Lepage's became the largest bakery in Maine.

The bakery paid me fifteen cents an hour, big money for me at the time. The five or six textile mills in Lewiston paid twenty-one cents an hour, but would not hire anyone under sixteen, per state law. So on my sixteenth birthday, I applied for a job at the Pepperel Bleachery, and was promptly hired. I worked there after school and weekends until I was seventeen.

On my seventeenth birthday, I enlisted in the U.S. Navy. That's another story.

108

LEWISTON, MAINE

2014

L ewiston, Maine, is the town where I was born in 1927 and the state's second largest city. Located in south central Maine, Lewiston has a population of about 36,000. At that time, my world was all of French-Canadian descent, with possibly a few Yanquees around the edges. All were Catholic in my world, except one Jew—an old man with a beard, whose old cart was pulled along by a hundred-year-old horse, with bones protruding, looking starved to death, and could hardly walk, but the infamous Jew would whip the hell out of it. That perfidious Jew was buying rags. He was yelling "rags," but most often he would yell "Guenilles! Guenilles! Guenilles et des claques!" Guenilles is French-Canadian for rags. Claques are rubbers to put on your shoes. This was during the depression in the early 1930s, followed by World War II when rubber was scarce. As soon as I could walk, and play in our front yard where Mother could watch me, as a street urchin with my friends, I would run after the wagon and yell at the Jew, "Who killed Christ? — Who killed Christ?" The old Jew would turn around, and try to reach us with his horsewhip. However, he whipped his old decrepit mare more often than any taunting boys, and once in a while a wayward girl also. Ah! We were so proud of it.

When the old Jew was lucky enough to hit a bad-mannered kid—which made him very happy and satisfied—all the French-Canadian Catholic families on the street would immediately canonize the sinful boy, until he was de-canonized by another perfidious youngster.

These are some of my memories from that time.

• • •

My first religious impression was in the evening after supper, when Dad would eat his late supper, while we had the family evening prayers. When I was still too young to walk or kneel, Mother rocked me in the rocking chair until I fell asleep. When she placed me in the bed, she recited out loud Au nom du Pere ("In the name of the Father").

• • •

As I grew up, Mother taught me the usual morning and evening prayers which I recited by my bed with clasped hands. Mother used to tell me I was a little angel. When I was old enough, I went to St. Peter's School, catty-corner from my home, where I was taught by the Dominican Nuns from Lyon, France. None of the nuns could speak English, except Mère Superieure (Mother Superior), who could always make herself understood, and not necessarily in English.

The best nun I recollect having is Mère Marie Jerome, and you will recollect her story as the peeing nun in my first book, *Monk to Bootlegger*. I never had a female teacher since. After fourth grade, I went on in a different division headed by the Brothers of the Sacred Heart from St. Hyacinthe, Canada. They were teaching brothers. My first male teacher was Brother Jean-Rosaire FSC. Oh, he was a good teacher and never lost his temper. Now we were grown up and could start learning English. Brother Jean-Rosaire taught us the English alphabet in French. You figure that one out! And it took the entire scholastic year to learn it.

St. Peter's Basilica 2014

The following year was my time to be an altar boy at St. Peter's. The large and beautiful church, which looked like a cathedral, is now a basilica. The Dominican Fathers from Canada were stationed there. Frère Méderic FSC taught me how to serve the masses—both low and high—in Latin. After I learned all my Latin prayers by rote, then I was ready for the movements. Oh! I loved to ring the bells at the sanctus. But I loved the cruets better. Those vessels were always under surveillance, when full. Yeah, surveillance of one kind or another—and not necessarily by authorized personnel.

My mother always told me I was an "early" child and I never fully understood that term, so I asked other kids in school. It's natural for kids in early school to ask each other the real meaning of sexual words. But an early birth, what does that mean? A kid in the grade above me finally said, "Dummy, it means you opened the door early." It has always satisfied me.

At St. Peter's, there were at least five masses every morning beginning at 5:00. I always insisted on serving the first mass of the day, and for good reason. We were paid five cents per mass served—big money for us, especially since it was during the Great Depression. Not too many boys loved to get up early, so they were often late or didn't show up at all. I was then available since I had just come off the altar. Then it was back to the altar again serving a different priest. Mother always taught me to save, so I saved some money in the two years I served mass. Boy, was I elated when I was finally able to open a $5.00 Christmas Savings Account!

I remained an altar boy for two years, an amount of time which later in life became my modus operandi. I was getting older, and it was time to be a paper boy (see chapter "Lewiston Sun & Journal").

Jerry at elementary school graduation

Today, sixty-five years later, you could well say, "The more Lewiston changes, the more it stays the same." Of course, many old buildings have been demolished to make way for new ones—on my recent trip, I saw that for myself. Yet change has to be expected.

A noticeable area of change is economic. When I was a youngster, economic mainstays were textile mills (where I worked part-time during World War II) and shoe shops (where my brother-in-law, Sam, worked). That is no longer true. However, the most visible changes are in demographics.

In the 1930s, as I was growing up, I knew of only one local black family, though I was told there might be two or three other families. I had never seen a black person until a black family from the South moved into Lewiston's middle income area. Their house had an unattached garage of fairly good size, and in it they opened a homemade ice cream shoppe. They became well off serving the Franco-Americans and Mainers of Irish descent. Although their ice cream was the very best in Lewiston, the reason many Lewistonians patronized the carryout shop was in order to see their first black family. The first time my mother took me there, I was amazed by the man who served us our pistachio ice cream. How the white of his eyes contrasted to his black skin! In my child's mind, I feared the ice cream I loved so much might be poisoned—and I turned it down!

• • •

At seventeen, I enlisted in the U.S. Navy and for the first time ever, I saw a nude black man. It was a novelty for me. I realized they are made the same way as the white man and all other races. The eye-opener granted me the realization that all men are created equal. Now, I was a real educated man.

• • •

THE SNOWSHOERS

In 1947, I founded Le Renard (The Fox) Snowshoe and Social Club. Our quarters were located on the corner of Lisbon and Chestnut Streets, Lewiston, Maine.

Le Renard building

We had a drum and bugle corps, well known for winning trophies in every parade. We practiced every Wednesday night in our hall on the second floor. It was a social event as well as a practice, and everyone looked forward to it.

As soon as the practice was over, I rushed to the sidewalk where Jeannine was waiting, and we would usually walk to my car next to the building on Chestnut—parked right under the street light, lest someone suspect hanky-panky.

Bosse, our drum major, was the boy (he was only fourteen) who really made our corps a success. At my age, I can't remember his first name, but when I went to Maine in October 2014 to visit Jeannine and my niece, Brenda, I asked old acquaintances if Bosse was still alive. No one knew.

He wore a striking, tall, drum major hat, with the head of a real black fox fastened to it; spectators would stretch their necks to get a good look at it. His baton twirling was always better than that of our competition. Once, his baton got caught in the overhead electrical lines crossing the street, and it made a splash, even in the newspapers. Seeking more publicity, I asked Bosse if he could replicate that event, but he had no luck despite several tries.

NOTA:

BOSSÉ, if you are still alive,
please contact me in Oklahoma!

My best friend ever, who helped me establish the club and its drum and bugle corps, was George Ricker, who then lived on Lincoln Street. After I left Lewiston and went on with my life, George went into politics at a rather young age. He loved to meet people, and never met a stranger. He was easily approachable and became a city alderman. After his death, the municipality of Lewiston dedicated a park in his honor.

Another great social snowshoer in our club was Lionel Potvin. He and I spent hours playing pool—honing our skills. After I left Lewiston, we lost contact, until 2014 when I learned a Lewiston city park had been named after him.

THE SOMALI BANTUS

The demographics of Lewiston have changed considerably since I left sixty-five years ago. Back then the black population was small, and even today Lewiston's American southern black population is still negligible. But that group is mightily outnumbered by the Somali Bantus. Even the description, Somali Bantus, is a misnomer to a certain degree. Apparently neither the U.S. legislators who passed the laws, nor our State Department who interpreted them, has made a study of foreign ethnicity.

Bantus are not ethnic Somalis; rather, they came to Somalia as slaves from countries to the south. Slavery was very common in those old days and cruelty was rampant. To the black Americans who love to harp on American slavery, simply read human history. There is a good documentary film on the Bantu and Somali which deals with this particular segment.

It is against the Muslim faith to own slaves, so the Bantus quickly converted after capture. Actually, the Bantus may be found mostly in the Somali south, where they are highly marginalized. They have never been Somalis, and neither are they now. They are called Somalis by the U.S. State Department because they lived within the confines of Somalia. Everything must be legal the American way, and damn the logic.

According to the last census, the Bantus of Lewiston are found in a thousand families which comprise 8.7% of the black population. Quite a contrast to the three or four black families I knew of as a boy. In Bantu language, the word Bantu means "people" or "humans."

In Somalia, the Bantus speak their own languages and not Somali. Within the Bantu tribes, there are from 300 to 600 separate ethnic groups, each with its own dialect. If you're seeking the Tower of Babel, look no further. The United Nations has rated Somalia's government as one of the most corrupt in the world.

In the 2010s, twenty-five Bantus from Lewiston went overseas to join ISIS in their fight for Muslim domination in the Middle East. One lost his life in the fight, and will never see Lewiston again. (Maybe he could not adapt to Lewiston, especially in the winter.)

For a people coming from the backwaters of a marginalized third world country, Bantus have adapted well to their new country. Their children are going to American schools, but lack complete fluency in English because they speak their own dialect at home. That situation has not changed since I was young. But the Bantu children appear to learn much faster than I did, for today I can have a decent conversation with Bantu children, while at their age, all I could speak was French. Standing in front of the house where I was born, I wondered if the Bantu children inside were sleeping in my old bed—at least that would be better than sleeping on the ground back in Somalia. I asked a variety of Bantu kids in my old front yard, "Are you Somali or Bantu?" Each child confirmed, "It's all the same, Somali or Bantu—no difference!" Uncle Sam, the media, and the Lewiston public had so brainwashed them they didn't even know their own ethnicity.

Bantu woman on Lisbon street

158 Blake Street

Jeannine and I came close to living together when were just babies. Well, not exactly, but here's the scoop:

The circled window indicates my bedroom from 1935 to 1945. My family was living in a (now-demolished) building (154 Blake Street) attached to the building shown in the photo. Coincidentally, Jeannine's family had resided in that same apartment building when she was born in 1935. But since her father had lost his job during the great depression, her family economized by moving down to Knox Street three blocks over—leaving just before my family rented that same apartment. So I'd guess you could classify that as a "missed connection." Incidentally, now at eighty-seven years old, I recall that the bed was still warm when I moved in it at the age of seven.

In this yard where the cars are parked, are so many happy memories, Bantu children are playing their own games. The entire neighborhood has gone Bantu. Yes, as I looked at the window where my bedroom is circled, I imagine the three Somali children I talked to in the street, sleeping in my old bedroom. It's rather comforting.

• • •

This white building and storefront is the Mogadishu Restaurant on Lisbon Street in Lewiston, Maine. Unfortunately, they do not serve beer. Nevertheless, I made many friends in the Bantu community here, and I even bought myself a set of Bantu Muslim clothes in that store. I wear these clothes in Oklahoma City when I go to the Istanbul or the Moroccan restaurants. It makes me feel at home.

Some Lewistonians resent the Bantus in their midst and openly wish they would go back home to Somalia. The fact is they have no home to go back to. They were not home and never felt at home in Somalia. Some good and wise men in the U.S. State Department realized this, and bulldozed legislation to bring them to the United States. These wise men then moved on to higher positions or the public sector, replaced by the normal government bureaucrats.

As a people, the Bantus have been displaced several times in every century of their existence, and that holds true for the twentieth and twenty-first century. Today they are trying to transcend two centuries in just a few years. The people of Lewiston can't understand why "the Somalis" may keep chickens in their homes. In the first place, they cannot identify these people properly. How can they be unprejudiced in their diagnosis? It borders on a travesty of justice.

RAY

Ray lived one block from me, on Pierce Street. I was nearly seventeen and he was almost two years older. I did not have a driver's license, but he did, and his older brother (a shoe salesman at Tom McCann) had a car. Three times, while I was a junior at St. Dominic's High School, we went to Boston on the weekend to see the show at the Old Howard. This was the top burlesque theater in New England, and it made us feel important to be able to go there, even though I was still underage. Simply watching the show made the sap run through my body, and I was always prepared, bringing with me an extra pair of boxer underwear. After the show, I would go to the men's room, and quickly change, crumple my dirty underwear, and place it in my pants pocket. Then I would nonchalantly rejoin Ray without saying a word. This is where my dichotomy of monk versus the world started. After two or three visits to the Old Howard, I turned seventeen and enlisted in the U.S. Navy.

• • •

World War II ended during my enlistment, and after serving twenty-three months, I was discharged. I arrived home the day after, and went to Pierce Street to see Ray. This time he dragged me downtown to enlist in a snowshoe club, where we had a beer. It was now the end of September, and the deer hunting season was starting in Maine. Ray suggested we go hunting, and of course I agreed. His brother had a Buick, a relatively large car in those days, with a large trunk. Ray borrowed his brother's rifle, so I borrowed my father's twelve-gage, twin-barrel shotgun.

Since I was two years Ray's junior, I easily took his lead. At 3 a.m. Saturday morning, we took off toward Canton, Maine. Arriving there at 4 a.m., we followed a dirt road off the edge of town, which ended in a dead end. Ray suggested we park there and stay in the car for an hour or two to let our eyes become accustomed to the dark. Then we'd be in good shape to start hunting before daylight.

After a while—which seemed like an eternity—Ray said, "I see shadows. We should go out now." Following his lead, I slid a slug in one barrel of the shotgun, and a buckshot in the other barrel. Soon the outline of a field appeared towards the end on the downgrade. I let my feet lead me wherever they would, and stopped often, observing all around me. Suddenly, I was at the edge of the woods. When I could see the outline of a small path in the woods, I began to follow it. It seemed I walked for an hour, but I probably traveled only two or three hundred feet. In the dark I tripped over some low rocks, which I later learned made up the wall of a small cemetery. Well, I sat on one of those stones to rest and wait for daybreak. My situation reminded me of the early morning watches I had aboard ship as I was returning from the Philippines.

I was becoming restless and uneasy when suddenly—BANG!

From the end of the field came the startling sound of a gunshot, but I had no time to react before all hell broke loose. Some kind of large animal appeared to be heading for the path I was in. As I watched, it became a moose with large antlers. Although the moose was approaching from afar, I dared not venture a shot, for there was no moose hunting season in Maine, and there were heavy penalties for those caught hunting them. But where did that shot come from?

My knees were shaking as I envisioned languishing in the Canton jail, the keys thrown away, and a hundred years later, my skeleton being released. I was brought back to my senses by trembling earth—the bull moose coming down the path at full gallop! With no time to think, my nerves took possession of me. I was in the center of the path; I tried to run, but my legs would not move. Everything began to happen in slow motion: I lifted the shotgun toward the moose coming down toward me a mile a minute. I would be dead if I didn't do something. In my gunsight, I saw the veins in his chest pumping blood. I aimed the slug where the two parts of the chest meet...and pressed the trigger. All I could hear was the rat-tat-tat of my knees knocking. The moose dropped to his knees, blood pouring out of his mouth. I tried to run, but my legs refused, my eyes transfixed the blood. Then the beast got to its feet and veered off to the side, barely thirty feet in front of me. I lifted the shotgun with only a gunshot in it... and let go a broadside. The animal fell down—deader than dead—blood all over its muzzle. Poor me...I tried to run away...but my legs would not move. I felt a thousand emotions in the space of a minute...then came calm—the calm of hell. Surely game wardens heard the shots... and would arrive in five minutes. I must get out of here! Visions...visions...visions!

All of a sudden, I heard voices—I listened intently—French-Canadian voices! What elation! I reasoned that a game warden in these parts would certainly not be French, and would be Yanquee! I was saved!

"Icite....Icite!" I began to relax as the French voices came closer. "I think it went down this path. Let's see!"

By that time I had walked up to the moose and grabbed its antlers. The French-Canadians spotted me at the same time I spotted them—and they ran for cover! I reacted likewise. After a few moments of stillness, we got up and began to approach each other. My shotgun was empty, but the rifles the three of them carried were apparently loaded.

One said, "I just shot this moose."

Instinctively, I retorted, "The hell you did, are you blind? These are buckshots on the side of the animal, and right there in his chest is my slug."

I pointed my empty shotgun toward that brave man who claimed to have shot the moose. There was an impasse for a few seconds.

Then a more somber head among them advised, "Let's all get together, cut a hindquarter, and get the hell out of here before a game warden arrives."

"Oh, no, you don't!" I shouted, suddenly being Mr. Level Head. "Not before I also get my hindquarter!"

"Fair enough!" all agreed. I had a sense they were neophytes in the woods and hunting—as I was! We proceeded to dismantle the hindquarters.

By that time Ray stumbled upon us–and promptly had a fit of apoplexy.

"Which of you is the crazy bastard that did this? I want no part of it. I'm getting out of here and returning to Lewiston!"

I got up on my haunches and told Ray, "No, you're not! Get back to your Buick, and drive down the field up to the path. In the meantime we're going to finish our job, and have the hindquarters waiting for you at the edge of the woods."

Ray started cussing and recited a litany of laws against killing moose, but I yelled, "Get out of here and get that Buick!"

One of the other Frenchies said to Ray, "My pickup is by your car, so I'll walk you up there."

Boy, what a relief. We had plenty of time to transport the two hindquarters to the edge of the field, where we waited impatiently for the two vehicles. During all this time, we had not necessarily become friends, as we were all on our guard. Mercifully, the vehicles arrived. It took three men on each of the hindquarters, so we all pitched in.

One man asked my name. I replied, "Levesque," and asked his. I don't remember his answer.

When the vehicles were loaded, we all took off in our various directions.

Of course Ray was my driver, and he whined all the way back to Lewiston. He was apparently a visionary: he could see a game warden at every curve in the road and behind every tree. The wardens would confiscate the Buick, throw him in jail, his brother would show up at the jail and kill him, there would be a long trial, and his brother would languish in the pen.

Ray drove straight to my house in Lewiston and told me in no uncertain terms to get that meat out of his car.

1937 Buick sedan

I had him drive by the basement window, but we needed another man to unload. By that time, Dad had seen us drive in and immediately guessed what we were doing. He came downstairs to help us!

We had just placed the hindquarter on the edge of the window when Ray let Dad have it. "Monsieur Levesque, your son is absolutely crazy. He will get us all in jail!"

"Come on, Ray, possess yourself!" Dad ordered. "Now get that car out of here."

We were all looking down the street anticipating the game wardens who were not there. A kindly neighbor helped Dad and me move the hindquarter to a safe place in the basement.

Dad and I walked upstairs, where I had to tell him the entire story.

"This is serious!" he said. "We must get the meat out of this house."

He and Mother talked over possibilities, and both agreed that Pete and Alice—our best family friends who lived at the edge of town—were our only recourse.

Mother called Alice, who, though reluctant, could not refuse to help us. Then Dad talked to Pete, who instructed him bring the meat over.

The hindquarter in the basement had to be lifted to the basement window. It would take two extra hands, but volunteers were there for the asking. The entire four floors of the apartment building knew about it, and everyone in the building was on the lookout on our behalf. We placed the moose meat in my father's car, and off to Fort Knox we went.

By the time we arrived at Pete's, even Alice was concerned about the law lurking behind every bush. Dad drove his car around Pete's house right up to the cellar storm door, but going down those stairs was tricky, so Pete's teenage son, Leo, helped us down the stairs. After our good-byes, Dad and I left.

Pete and Alice ready to leave for their honeymoon

For the following two weeks, we received game warden reports every day—from the entire neighborhood! We all held down the fort.

In the evenings after work, Dad would drive to Pete's to carve wonderful moose steaks for both families. Dad made hamburger meat, and Mother showed Dad which cuts she wanted to make mincemeat, preserving dozens of jars. For an entire year, both families had the best mince pies in New England. However, till the day she died, Alice never forgave me for killing that moose, and endangering the loss of her house. Pete and Dad passively looked on, never saying a word.

Years went by and the issue was forgotten—seemingly.

• • •

Some years later, I happened to be in Lewiston in between escapades, when the telephone rang and I found with great surprise and pleasure that it was Leo Dick.

Dick had been a fellow member of Le Renard "The Fox" snowshoe social club. In 1950, when the Korean War started, Dick joined the mighty U.S. Marine Corps for the regular enlistment span of four years.

"Jerry, I'm on leave for a few days! Can we meet for a beer tonight?" After Dick served for three years, the Marines had given him two weeks leave to encourage him to reenlist.

In half an hour, we met at Dick's house, where we embraced as two prodigal chums, complete with back-thumping and the coarse nautical language that only U.S. Navy and U.S. Marines can utter.

We drifted down to a small, popular place on Knox Street that we had enjoyed once before. The unique tavern was built like a railroad car.

As we entered, the only other patrons were a table of four men enjoying their beers at the farthest end. We sat three tables away and ordered a beer. Dick began bragging on how tough the Marines were as compared to the swabbies. I knew it was only bravado, so I kept quiet, all the while cocking my ear to listen to the four men down the way. They were dressed as hunters, and the conversation was about hunting. Suddenly, I picked up on the word "moose" and shushed Dick to listen to that conversation with me.

One man was doing all the talking, while the other three listened in rapt attention. Then I realized he was talking about my moose. When I shot the moose several years before, I didn't know these hunters were from Lewiston. Now—two and two makes four—I learned it quickly. In a split second, I was infused with the emotions of gladness, hurt, despair, and more. Then the man said, "And I shot the S.O.B."

My blood boiled, my face reddened—I could hardly believe my ears!

In a hoarse but indignant whisper, I told Dick, "What a fricking liar! I am the man who shot that moose!"

Dick grabbed the ball and ran with it. "Really? Let's go clean their clocks, and throw them out of the diner!"

We both got up and walked up to the table. Putting on the most authoritative mien I could muster, I addressing myself to the so-called shooter. Leaning over him, I said, "Mister, who shot that moose?"

The man was taken aback and began scrutinizing me, but I didn't give him time to reply. In my most kingly stance, I thumped my own chest and answered for him: "I did!"

The eager Dick whispered to me, "Time to wipe them out, huh?"

"Shuh...shuh...Dick."

By then, all four men, embarrassed and fearful, "saw the light."

I told Dick, "They're caught with their pants down, so that's enough. Let's get the hell out of here."

All riled up and no place to go, Dick protested, but I dragged him out of the diner.

That was the last I saw or heard of Leo Dick.

(FAST SKIP TO 2014)

In 2014, I took a two-week vacation to Maine and stopped by to see Leo Gagne, a friend since childhood. As we reminisced, Leo told me, "When your dad died, I was given that moose-killing shotgun, and I sold it for $400." I was incredulous. That gun wasn't worth one dollar, since it was made of blue steel—forbidden by law in Maine—for it could explode in your face. If the wardens or police saw it, they would confiscate it. Leo, now 82, said, "I knew it all the time and kept quiet."

While visiting Leo Gagne, we also walked next door to visit his neighbor, Norm Garand. I've known Norm since the drum and bugle corps days at Le Renard Club, but haven't seen him since the summer of 1950, the Korean War. Those of you who have my first book, *Monk to Bootlegger*, look at the Renard Drum and Bugle Corps photo on page 65: Norm Garand is the last man on the right, kneeling.

WORLD WAR II

Just before the beginning of World War II, the United States Government required all men of a certain age to register at a draft board close to their home. As training facilities became available, young men were periodically called by their draft boards into active military service.

The young men were going to war. Factories sprang up all over the United States and most high schools rearranged class hours to allow students to work a few hours a day in a war factory. At age fourteen, I took an afternoon and early evening job in a bakery, and at sixteen I went to work in a textile factory producing herringbone twill cloth for army uniforms. Most of my friends were a year or two older than I, and I enlisted in the naval reserve on my seventeenth birthday. When I got home I presented my enlistment papers to my parents for their signatures. Of course, they refused because, for years, they had their minds set on sending me to the seminary to become a priest. Still I begged and begged my parents to sign my papers.

I had learned that whatever I wanted, I should take the means to make it happen. So I simply stopped turning in my assignments or going to school. When family friends and relatives found out I was not going to school, my parents were humiliated beyond belief, and agreed to sign. Voila!

> Ask not what your country
> can do for you,
> Ask what you can do
> for your country!
>
> *Inaugural Address*
> *John F. Kennedy*
> *January 1961*

I have always been very religious and patriotic—often way ahead of my time. The words above were spoken by Jack Kennedy at his inaugural address, eighteen years after I enlisted, and they still ring in my ears.

Thanks to the Dominican nuns and the Brothers of the Sacred Heart, who, early on, instilled in my heart, the love of God and Country.

In upper New York State, I completed my boot camp, after which the Navy selected 300 sailors for a spelling test. The top thirty men would be sent to San Francisco to undergo three months of mailman training. Even though I could not hold a fluent conversation in English, the Brothers who taught me at St. Dominic's High School in Lewiston had made sure we were proficient in spelling.

The Navy gave us "subsistence pay," meaning we had to find our own living quarters in San Francisco while going to mailman school. Three other sailors and I chose a boarding house with a large room adjacent to Buena Vista Park as our home for the three months of schooling. After graduating, we were declared Petty Officer Third Class with a Mailman rating and shipped to Manila in the Philippines where we were to establish a fleet post office.

Our work consisted of receiving incoming mail from the United States or anyplace else, sorting it out by ship name, unit, etc., and routing it on to its final destination. This was the tail end of World War II, and thousands of United States ships were in the far east at that time; thus mailmen were sorting mail twenty-four hours a day.

We arrived in Manila right after the city was liberated from the Japanese and secured. Instead of setting up tents, kitchens, and latrines, the Navy pulled a floating barge "hotel" with all amenities up the Pasig river in Manila, and anchored it just south of Jones Bridge. A Quonset building was quickly built where we could sort the mail, protected from Manila's daily rain showers. Hundreds of mail bags came and went each day and we often "borrowed" Japanese prisoners of war to handle these bags, thus releasing the Navy mailmen to sort the mail. The Prisoners of War were glad to work on these details, for it gave them an opportunity to learn English, eat better food than in the camps, and snag an occasional soft drink or cigarette.

Our working camp was on a narrow strip of land about eighty feet wide between the Pasig River and Intramuros, an old, walled university grounds built centuries ago by the Spaniards. The walls were thick and strong, having withstood canon fire from the Spaniards and the United States centuries ago, and from the Japanese in World War II. We quickly found a ladder to set up against the wall, and often climbed over the wall to walk on university grounds. One day as I was walking the extensive streets on the other side of the wall, I saw a manhole cover being pushed up from the street, and a man crawled out of the hole and sat on the edge. Immediately, Filipinos jumped toward the man, yelling something in Tagalog, the native language which I didn't understand. The man turned out to be a Japanese soldier who had been hiding in the labyrinth of tunnels under the city for six months. When he ran out of food, he surrendered. The military police took him into custody, fed him, debriefed him, and placed him in a prisoner of war camp.

Intramuros gate before World War II

Sherman tank bursting through Intramuros wall, 1945

YAMASHITA

In early 1945, Japanese General Yamashita commanded all Japanese Army troops in the northern Philippines. In September, he surrendered to American troops, and two months later was on trial for his life.

I was fortunate enough to attend the trial for one week in December 1945. It was an experience never to be forgotten by a sailor just turned eighteen.

In 1946, Yamashita was found guilty of Japanese atrocities, and died by hanging.

General Yamashita surrenders

As soon as the war was over, draftees and reservists were transferred back to the states and discharged. I had been in Manila nine months, and as a reservist, it was my turn to be discharged. Although I was only eighteen years old, I already felt like an old man.

KOREAN WAR

The Korean War started June 25, 1950, and being in the United States Naval Reserve, I received a telegram directing me to report at the Portland, Maine, Naval Station within forty-eight hours. The navy assigned me to serve on a destroyer stationed in Newport, Rhode Island, and I reported there that very evening. Papers in hand, I boarded the ship, only to be told not to unpack, for I was being sent to navy schools. The schooling covered grid map reading, shore fire control, codes, and portable radio operations. After six months of intense training, seven days a week, I returned to the ship on January 2, 1951. The *William R. Rush* was commanded by Captain Harold Hamlin Jr. from Maine and a long line of seafaring men. The executive officer was Commander Audley S. McCain USN, the uncle of Senator John McCain. At that time, our McCain's brother, who also was an officer in the USN, was commander in chief of the Pacific fleet.

On January 3, 1951, the *William R. Rush* sailed for the Far East. Steaming via the Panama Canal, Pearl Harbor, Midway (where we saw the gooney birds), and Sasebo, Japan. On this leg of the trip, we had battle stations drill every day. McCain was in charge of these drills, and he was very demanding. Being the ship's mailman, I had no battle station. Once that came to McCain's attention, he quickly placed me in radio shack, monitoring voice traffic. When we heard ALL HANDS, MAN YOUR BATTLE STATIONS, all swabs ran to their battle stations on the double. Since at first, I had no battle station, I was excess baggage in the radio shack, so I would closet myself in the radio equipment compartment.

Midshipman Audley Hill McCain
Photo thanks to Bill Gonyo

One day during a drill, McCain came looking for me. He had paperwork in his hand, and asked all the radio men in radio shack, "Where is Frenchie? My list says he is supposed to be here!" No one answered. McCain saw the closed door of the radio equipment compartment. I was on the other side of that hatch, sleeping on the hard steel deck. McCain pushed the hatch to open it, but ran into resistance. My feet were obstructing the door.

I felt someone trying to push the hatch door. Being half asleep, I figured no one in radio shack had any business disturbing me, so I gave the door a great big kick. As I kicked, I heard McCain say, "Frenchie? Frenchie? Is that you, Frenchie?" As I finished my kick, I realized I had almost caught McCain's nose between the door and bulkhead. I almost doo-dooed in my pants, but I got up immediately and faced the music.

McCain was red as a tomato. "Frenchie, I see this is not the place for you. I am going to reassign you to Plot." The Plotting Room is the compartment where they control the ship's fire. I had never been inside this compartment, as most sailors were kept away from that area.

On the next drill, I ran to Plot, and my buddies showed me the gyrocompass: It's like a carpenter's level and when the captain ordered "FIRE," I was to watch the little bubble until it became level, and only then should I quickly pull the trigger. It is then, and only then that I realized I was controlling every missile we shot at the enemy. I had gone from being a real flunkie, to having just about the most important job on the ship during battle. We subsequently joined Task Force 77 in Korean waters.

USS William R. Rush at anchor. Circa early 1950s. Courtesy of Joseph Koye (1930-1984)

When we arrived at the coast of North Korea, ship orders called for the interdiction (prevention) of enemy railroad traffic along the coast.

We took a position close to a railroad tunnel and the captain figured we would wait for the train to come up the coast and then bottle it up in the tunnel by destroying the entrance. This we did, but we were never told the results of that night's bombardment.

On April 14, 1951, the Rush was assigned patrol duty in the Formosa Straights near the coast of China to prevent probable invasion forces from crossing the China Sea and overrunning Formosa.

The President of Free China, Chiang Kai-Shek, had fled free China with the few ships he had and we did not think the remaining communists had any ships at that time. Our ship made a leisurely patrol. Captain Hamlin often took potshots with a high powered rifle at the sharks swimming near our ship. Sometimes the sharks would jump clearly out of the water, to our amusement. It was a popular pastime for the sailors, and the captain was cheered when he made a hit.

We were the only ship on that patrol for a week. We even had the opportunity for a shore leave in Keelung, a port on northwest Formosa (Taiwan). Five or six of us rented a car and headed for the capital. During our trip, several police motorcycles going in the opposite direction waved us over, telling us to stay put until dignitaries had passed.

After about ten minutes, a convoy of cars appeared, surrounded by motorcycles. Chinese policemen on motorcycles saluted the convoy. Our driver told us it was Chiang Kai-Shek himself, in a large black American-made Buick. I recognized the Buick but couldn't see inside its black curtains.

After a week of the Formosa patrol, the ship headed to Sasebo, Japan, for badly needed repairs, logistics, and recreation for the crew.

On May 29, the Rush was assigned duties as the bombing line destroyer off the front lines of Korea, operating vigorously in direct support of United Nations troops ashore. Bombardments were conducted on thirty-three separate occasions, expending hundreds of rounds of ammunition on targets such as towns, bridges, bivouac areas, railroads, motorized transports, direct support of troops, and interdiction firing. On two occasions the Rush assisted friendly troops to escape "miniature Dunkirks" from the beaches into sampans and junks when South Korean troops were overwhelmed by larger forces. This was at the time when the Chinese communists crossed the Yalu River between China and North Korea and entered the war to regain the North. It's not that they had modern arms, they simply had overwhelming manpower and employed them in human waves, pushing the South Koreans and Americans back to the prewar demarcation lines. The accurate heavy fire by the Rush forced the enemy to retire inland. As my battle station was in Plot, imagine, I was the trigger man for all those missiles fired from our ship.

In June, the enemy returned with overwhelming force. The devastating and accurate fire delivered by the Rush brought praise from all quarters. It is said that when communist troops leave their rice behind they are usually in a hurry, and that particular night they left everything behind. The firing at times was as close as 150 yards from United Nations troops. The efforts of the Rush produced such spectacular results that the commanding general of the 11th Republic of Korea Division, Brigadier General Oh Duk Jun, at his own request, came aboard and presented the ship with scrolled citations from several ROK commanders. This ceremony took place on board ship offshore at the front lines.

On June 13, 1951, the Rush completed her duties in the Far East, and on June 17 we set sail for the return trip to the United States.

Joseph when his ship was in dry dock in Yokasuka, Japan

The highlight of our return trip was crossing the equator. It is tradition aboard U.S. Navy ships crossing the equator, that any sailors aboard ship who have never passed the equator must be initiated in an elaborate ceremony. The ship lies still and just floats on the ocean. Everything comes to a halt. The old timers dress up as King Neptune (hardly any dress) and his court. The fattest man in the crew is usually chosen as King Neptune, especially if he has a big belly! The belly is first rubbed with a good thickness of gear grease, and all new pollywogs are made to kneel in front of King Neptune while a sailor behind him pushes his head on the belly. The pollywog, his face and hands full of grease, must then stand at attention and hear a proclamation before he is free to hose down and take a shower below. This scene was so ethereal, I ran to my quarters, grabbed my Kodak movie camera, and shot the entire ceremony.

• • •

The author in Hong Kong

Ports of call included Hong Kong with its rickshaws, Singapore, and Ceylon (now Sri Lanka). We had the opportunity to visit the Temple of the Tooth (the tooth of Buddha), to climb onto the back of decked-out elephants, and to participate in an elegant parade honoring Buddha.

Oh! It was hot!

We sailed past the southern tip of India to Ras Tanura in the Persian Gulf. (Ras Tanura means "Cape Oven" due to the unusual heat at this cape.) The Persian Gulf close to shore is so shallow we had to anchor far offshore. The captain told me we had lots of mailbags waiting for us ashore, and he authorized me to select a work crew of three men to help. One of the sailors was Henri Desrosiers of Worcester, Masssachusetts, a fellow New Englander and Franco-American. In most ports around the world, embarking as a work crew also means a chance for a quick stop in a pub—but never in Saudi Arabia. We were guests of the Saudi Arabian Oil Company (ARAMCO) and the government of Saudi Arabia. Departing from the ship in a small motor whaleboat were two work crews, one to get provisions and one to get mail. The gulf was slightly choppy that day, and all of a sudden, porpoises were leading us in—a sign of good luck. Rubbing against the sides of our small wooden boat, the porpoises appeared to be giants, at least larger than others we had seen in various oceans. I was sitting close to the edge of the boat and placed my right hand in the water. A wild porpoise actually brushed against my arm and I felt the entire length of its body. Another thrill of a lifetime!

The author at Ras Tanura

We were shepherded on a bus driven by a Saudi dressed in the traditional Saudi flowing desert robe and headdress—my first sight of a real Arab outside the movie *Beau Geste* on a Saturday afternoon when I was a child. (*Beau Geste* was the precursor to the film *Lawrence of Arabia*.) After driving only a few minutes, the bus stopped, the driver took out his prayer mat, spread it on the sand, and prayed to Allah—one of the five Muslim obligatory prayers of the day. (Incidentally, Catholic monks pray at least seven times a day.) We waited ten minutes for the driver to resume our short trip. I quickly learned that whenever it is prayer time, wherever they are, the Saudis will stop and proceed to their prayers without bother or *"souci."*

We stayed anchored off Ras Tanura overnight, then sailed back through the Straits of Hormuz, the Gulf of Aden, and up through the Red Sea. Really, all you see on each side are sand dunes. One evening's visit to Port Said, Egypt, proved to us how tightly packed Arab cities can be, and it was there I was first introduced to the gyro. Little did I foresee that in the evening of my life, gyros would become my favorite food.

As we left the Middle East heading for Europe, everyone aboard knew we would be hitting a port in France, so they all wanted to learn French, and then to practice what they had learned. Some would go to the other Frenchie on board (Desrosiers) and others to me, Frenchie the Mailman, to be taught. It was always the same drill: "Mademoiselle, voulez-vous coucher avec moi ce soir?" ("Mademoiselle, will you sleep with me tonight?") I'll never know where they picked up that phrase—it could have been from that other Frenchie, but it certainly didn't come from me.

Desrosiers, the other Frenchie

Another overcrowded city was Naples. — Ah, Naples! — Pizza di Napoli! Mama mia! Two of us rented a horse-drawn buggy to tour the crowded city. I took lots of movies with my camera, then placed it on the floor of the buggy between my two feet to protect it. There were tall buildings, narrow streets, and many street urchins shouting "Hello, Joe!"—all G.I.'s were Joe to them, G.I. Joe. Everywhere I turned, a dirty little hand was extended, begging for our attention. At first my heart went out to each one, but later I did my best to ignore them and protect my billfold. There was so much going on, I was flabbergasted. In no time, I realized my expensive movie camera was gone. So much for my tour of Naples.

Marseilles also had a large Muslim population, mostly Algerians from North Africa. Two of us took an autobus to Aubagne, the home of the French Foreign Legion. I was looking for Beau Geste, which I remembered from Saturday afternoon movies as a small boy. When we saw the Foreign Legion accompanied by their marching band—an impressive sight indeed—I got goose pimples.

Foreign Legionnaires

We spent a few hours on Gibraltar, long enough to see the baboons climbing on the Rock, then steamed across the Atlantic Ocean back to our home port, Newport, Rhode Island. That ended my year of Korean War service. I have never regretted it.

Uncle Sam had been good to me. Thanks be to God.

SOUTH KOREAN CITATION

Col. Chae Suk Yong coming aboard the USS William R. Rush DD-714

TRANSLATION OF SCROLL CITATION

From: Col. Chae Suk Yong, Commanding 13th Infantry Regiment
               11th Division, Army of the Republic of Korea
To: USS William R. Rush (DD-714)

Your ship has come to the Republic of Korea in the sacred cause of keeping the peace of the world, and it has served that cause bravely.

Our 13th Regiment, of the 11th Division, took over the front-line position at the East coast of Korea on May 30th, 1951. Since that time your heavy and accurate fire on enemy forces, day and night, has brought complete frustration to the enemy's plans for a spring offensive and has inflicted heavy casualties.

In particular, on the night of June 7th at about 2000 an enemy force of about one regiment of North Koreans attacked our regiment position. Largely through the aid of your powerful bombardment, we were able to rout the enemy completely, and advance to a more favorable position.

Such stalwart help will linger in glorious memory—not only in our regimental history, but in the whole history of our republic.

This testimonial is rendered to you in praise of your glorious achievement.

Submitted by William "Bill" Hammen, EM2/c,1950-51

MONTREAL

Aunt Jeanne and Uncle Hermenegilde Nadeau lived in Montreal ever since their 1920 wedding. Most of their seven children were born, brought up, and schooled in Montreal, and all of them were very industrious.

ROGER: In the late 1930s, the oldest boy, Roger, was involved in Canadian politics and helped found a new political party. Although Roger was quite liberal by our standards, the others in his circle were even more so. After two or three years, he realized the "others" were communists attempting to lead their party in that direction, and Roger dropped them like a hot potato.

After that experience, Roger founded an information bureau of sorts, and sold membership fees. The members could call or write the bureau to find answers to their questions, whatever they might be. Members included doctors, industrialists, teachers, or simply average citizens. I am told he was very successful at it, and it was growing by leaps and bounds. In all his research, he became convinced he could make more money as a private investigator. So after World War II, he sold his information bureau and became Roger Nadeau, imminent Private Investigator.

Two or three years afterward, a prominent French-Canadian woman was murdered in Florida, where many Canadians have been retiring for years. There was a trial with international publicity, and Roger was retained by the murdered woman's family to do his part. I never knew the particulars, except that the Floridians would have no part of a high-pressure Canadian investigator, so Roger returned to Montreal empty-handed. That was in the late 1950s and was the last I've heard of Roger.

ROBERT: The second boy in the family was Robert Nadeau. At the beginning of World War II Camilien Houde (see *Monk to Bootlegger*), then Mayor of Montreal, exhorted all French-Canadian young men to take to the woods in order not to be drafted to fight for the British—such was the animosity of French-Canadians for the British. So Robert, in his late teens, immediately took to the north Canadian woods. Two years later, he came home to Montreal under cover of darkness, but he was promptly denounced by a neighbor and arrested by the police. He was sent to an army training camp where, the first time he was given a rifle and live ammunition, he shot himself in the foot so as not to serve overseas.

During the last year of the war, Robert spent several months visiting my parents in Lewiston while I was serving in the U.S. Navy in the Far East. He was sleeping in my bed during that time. I was not fighting for the British, I was fighting for the United States, and always had great respect for Britain's contributions in World War I and World War II.

After the war, Robert acquired a large resort in North Hatley, Quebec, which contained a hundred guest rooms, a general restaurant, facilities for three simultaneous weddings with banquet facilities, dance floors and bandstands. It also had a swimming pool, and a well-known summer theater.

MAURICE: The third boy in the family, Maurice Nadeau, was born in Bidderford, Maine, and studied to be a Franciscan priest. The day after his ordination he went on a tour of New England with his father and mother to visit his relatives. We were first on his itinerary, and the Nadeaus were at our house only half a day. My folks had managed to save $100 as a gift towards Friar Maurice's chalice—that was big money in the early 1940s. Our two proud families were in the living room, congratulating the new friar on his chosen vocation. His father, Herman, had been gassed by the Germans in World War I, and all the relatives said that Herman had not been "quite right" ever since. But now he was a successful Montreal jeweler with the personality of a high-pressure auto salesman. My father always looked askance at Herman.

As the two families were basking in the ordination event, Father felt it was the proper time to present his gift to the new Franciscan. But at that precise moment, Uncle Herman brought up the fact that Maurice had taken the vows of Poverty, Chastity, and Obedience. That's why Franciscans have three knots on the rope around their loins, and they practice the Vow of Poverty in its full meaning. So Franciscans would not touch money at all, but he, Herman, would do so—for his son—and would keep the books. When I noticed my father's elongated face, I thought, What is he thinking now? Is he in a muddle?

Dad produced the crisp, new hundred dollar bill, and with Friar Maurice looking on, presented it to his brother-in-law, Uncle Herman.

The new priest served in the Franciscan Order for nine years, and had the privilege of serving in Japan and Hawaii before leaving the priesthood. In 1963, he married Samiko Yamamoto, a Buddhist in Hawaii, and converted to Catholicism at that time. I am told that Maurice took a position with the Canadian Immigration Service, and worked his way up to become a high official in the department. They had four beautiful children of mixed race, and lived happily ever after.

GERARD: The fourth boy was my age, and carried the same baptismal name. The name given me at birth was Gerard, which I used throughout my school years, but the day I entered the Navy at seventeen, and presented my birth certificate, my name was shown to be Joseph Gerard, and ever since I have been known as Joseph Levesque.

Gerard Nadeau attended the Washington Catholic University and earned his doctorate in chemistry. He joined the Brothers of Christian Instruction (La Mennais), who sent him to Africa as a missionary teacher. Later, he set up the chemistry department in the first college to be erected in the country of Uganda. After twenty years in Africa, he returned to Canada for a sabbatical and spent a summer with his brother Robert at the North Hatley Inn, working as its bartender during that time. On the first of September that year, his vacation time was up and he was asked to report at his order's mother house. On his way there, he died in an automobile accident. He was forty-four years old.

PAULINE: The fifth child of Aunt Jeanne and Uncle Herman was Pauline. She was the Nadeau sibling I knew best as a child. My mother took my sister and me back to Ham-Nord every summer until age ten or twelve, and Aunt Jeanne would bring Pauline along with her. Pauline was always full of pep and vinegar, and we children enjoyed spending our summers with her for a decade.

After her schooling in Montreal, Pauline became a nun and was sent as a missionary sister to Sri Lanka. I lost track of her after that.

NORMAND: The sixth child in that family was Normand. After his schooling in Montreal he became a tour guide at St. Joseph's Oratory in Montreal. One day while Normand was conducting a tour, a tourist turned crazy and stabbed him right on the steps of this famous shrine. He died on the spot.

MARCEL: The seventh child was Marcel. After his studies, he became a lay Catholic missionary in the headwaters of the Amazon in South America. He wrote several letters home about his travels. Marcel reported that one day he was in a small boat on the Amazon when a Franciscan missionary fell overboard. Before the others could help him, the piranhas devoured him in seconds right before their eyes.

While in Peru, Marcel contracted leprosy and was sent back to Canada, where he settled in Vancouver. He heard of the great reputation of the American leprosarium in Carville, Louisiana, and asked to be sent there for treatment. He was told, "No, Canada takes care of its own." That's the last I've heard of Marcel.

CARMEN: The eighth and last child in the family was Carmen. Being older than she was, I did not get to know her well. I understand she is still living in Granby, Quebec, where she has been a Realtor all her working life.

ST. JOSEPH'S ORATORY

By the grace of god, Brother Andre Besette is responsible for the existence of the world-renowned chapel known as St. Joseph's Oratory. He entered the Congregation of Holy Cross in 1870, and a year later was given a succession of duties to test his vocation. In 1878, he was credited with healing the sick and infirm by applying oil from a devotional lamp in the Chapel of St. Joseph. He has always credited his healings to the intercession of St. Joseph. Word of his healings spread all over the world.

In 1896, his congregation acquired land on the mountain facing the college, and Brother Andre soon realized his dream—of establishing a new chapel dedicated to St. Joseph on that new land. After forty years at the college of his order, he was appointed guardian of the oratory in 1934. Pilgrims by the millions came to pray for his intercession.

In 1934, for my seventh birthday, my parents took me to Montreal where we visited with Brother Andre for close to ten minutes. I remember him as being a simple and holy man, jovial and easy to talk to. For my birthday present, Mother purchased a black rosary from him for one dollar; prior to that, I had never received such an expensive gift. I still have it today, after eighty years.

Saint Andre Bessette, C.S.C.

When Brother Andre died in 1937—at the age of ninety-one—a million people came to pay their respects: the casket was viewed for six days. The oratory is now Canada's largest church. The dome was designed by a priest of his order, and is the third largest dome of its kind in the world. Even today, two million visitors and pilgrims visit the oratory each year.

In 2010, Brother Andre was canonized by Pope Benedict XIV, and is now Saint Andre of Montreal.

CHAPTER 2

MONASTERIES

FOUNDATION

The 1950s saw the emergence of secular institutes, which received much publicity in Catholic publications. These entities were to be the new form of dedication—without the accoutrements and the high structure of religious communities. Curious, I drove to Hannibal, Missouri, where such an institute was in the process of being formed. The priest founder was a hospital chaplain with high ideals and vision, yet with no specific apostolate and no prospective members—it puzzled me.

The following morning, another onlooker by the name of Marcus Medrano presented himself. I could see he was as confused as I was. Being in the same boat, we quickly became acquainted. Since the facility had invited us to stay overnight, we spent most of the day questioning its representatives. That evening, Marcus and I exchanged ideas regarding what we had learned.

When Joseph Marling, bishop of the Diocese of Jefferson City, dropped in the next morning to say hello to the chaplain of the facility, we were introduced to him. Marcus and I told Bishop Marling of our aspirations to join a community of "working" brothers. Because a secular institute did not satisfy our individual requirements, we expressed regret that we each must return to our respective homes.

The bishop picked up on our not-so-subtle message. "We are a new diocese and badly in need of such a community in different works."

I explained that I would love to work in a Catholic cemetery, which would coincide with my religious ideals.

"Choose any cemetery you want in the diocese," he said, "but remember we also need you more in other works," some of which he began to name. Then he asked me, "What would you name the new community?"

Ah! His name was Joseph also, so, inspired, I answered, "The Brothers of Saint Joseph, after the patron of cemetery workers, and all workers; and the patron of a happy death."

"Good choice! Do you have a checking account? Do you have money?"

"No, only enough for gas to return home to Maine."

Bishop Marling produced his checkbook on the spot, instructing me to go to a certain bank in downtown Hannibal (the home of Mark Twain) and open a checking account under the name of Brothers of St. Joseph. He wrote a check for $500. The bishop had made us an offer we could not refuse, and Marcus opted to stay also.

The diocese was opening a new minor seminary in an old school building, and already making repairs. Bishop Marling asked Marcus and me if we would work there temporarily to expedite the school opening two months later.

One month later, the building was ready for school. Late on a Friday afternoon, the bishop arrived unannounced. After a short conversation, we discerned he was hungry. Marcus opened a can of baked beans—the first meal served in this building under the auspices of the diocese.

As we ate, Bishop Marling looked up from his baked beans. "Marcus, would you cook for the seminary?" Marcus confirmed that he would.

Then the bishop turned to me. "We need someone to maintain this building seven days a week. Will that be you?"

That settled it. Our work was cut out for us. That evening, the bishop called the prospective seminarians to announce the opening of the seminary two days hence.

The rector and two teachers arrived the next day, and the seminary opened the following day—three months late. There were twenty-five students, all fourteen and fifteen years old. I was to maintain the building, keep floors clean and polished, stoke the coal furnace in the winter, and do everyone's laundry.

The students had school five and a half days per week. After dinner, they had recreation, study period for an hour, and then a chapel service capping their busy day with the rosary, vespers, and the Salve Regina.

The three priest teachers were not especially fond of their evening duty: supervising the recreation, the study period, and the prayer services. Each one came to me asking for relief from his heavy load. They had to prepare the next day's classes, perform other duties, and besides they had a social life—helping in parishes and visiting the sick. I absolutely refused to supervise the recreation, as I had enough to do in the laundry after dinner, but I agreed to take the study period, which would provide me with an opportunity to rest and do a little study of my own. In contrast with public school students, these students were always very courteous.

The author visits with seminarians before evening study period

Marcus and I had been given a large, empty classroom as our bedroom. He placed his bed in a corner, and mine was catty-corner, with a table in the center. The chapel services were really made for us, and we attended every night without fail. After services, Marcus would make a walk-by of the kitchen to make sure everything was secure. I checked both front and back doors, and the basement door. In the cold months, I stoked the furnace before returning to our sleeping room. Marcus would typically be sitting at the table, waiting for me to recite the rosary.

"But we just said the rosary half an hour ago," I said.

"Yes, Joseph, but this one is for us, to ask God's blessings on our community."

I soon found out there were no cemeteries in this diocese large enough to support a community of brothers, frugal though we were, so it was time to move on. Marcus despaired but returned to Denver, where he started and ran his own furniture refinishing company for a few years, and then entered a seminary.

After I consulted with Bishop Marling, he made a phone call to Lafayette, Louisiana, and arranged for me to be named manager of Calvary Cemetery. I sometimes wondered if I owed obedience to the bishop of Jefferson City in Missouri or to the bishop of Lafayette, Louisiana, but I never asked.

SÉNANQUE

Sénanque Abbey

S énanque is a Cistercian Abbey in Provence, France, founded in 1148 by Cistercian monks. Temporary huts housed the first impoverished monks but the community grew quite fast. By 1152 the community had so many members some of the monks were sent elsewhere to found another community.

The young community found patrons in the surrounding Lords, enabling them to build an abbey church, consecrated in 1178. This is now considered a national monument as one of the finest examples of Romanesque architecture existing in France. It consisted of the abbey church, cloister, dormitory, chapter house, and a small calefactory, the only heated space in the abbey where the monks could warm up in cold weather or where they could write, and thus was also called the scriptorum. The abbey is a remarkably untouched survival of rare beauty and severity.

There were no beds in those days. The monks would simply sleep on the floor dressed in their habits. The house Rules stipulated the amount of space for each monk. They were unable to cozy to each other for warmth on cold days. It was against the Rule.

Dormitory

In the thirteenth and fourteenth centuries, Sénanque reached its apogée with four flour mills and seven granges, and possessed large estates in Provence. Then the community went into decline. By 1509, the group had shrunk to about a dozen. During the Wars of Religion, the abbey was ransacked by Huguenots, some of whom might have been my ancestors (see *Monk to Bootlegger*). During the French Revolution (1789-1799), the abbey's lands were nationalized, and the one remaining monk was expelled; Sénanque itself and all its properties were sold to private individuals, as were most monasteries in France. This was one way for the new government to support itself.

The site was repurchased in 1854 by a benefactor for a new community of Cistercian monks, and Cistercians have inhabited the abbey off and on, ever since. The monks who live at Sénanque today grow lavender and tend honeybees for their livelihood.

Two other early Cistercian abbeys in Provence are Silvercane Abbey and Le Thoronet Abbey; together with Sénanque, they are sometimes referred to as the "Three Sisters of Provence."

Inner cloister of the abbey

When my former abbot in Canada was appointed prior of Our Lady of Nazareth, he was prior in Sénanque (see *Monk to Bootlegger*). His spirit and devotion is what I was trying to emulate in The Brothers of St. Joseph. Obviously, I was a failure, but life must go on.

I visited Sénanque three times in the 1980s, and once during flowering time for the lavender, I walked in the rows of flowers breathing all that fragrance. I was so glad and so touched by the colors, I looked around me and, seeing no one, I threw myself on the lavender as if I were going to bed.

Alas, almighty God sees everything—in the person of a brother monk, who went bananas when he saw me swimming in my new bed. He remonstrated with me, and promptly showed me the way out.

Au revoir.

Back in Oklahoma, two months later, one morning I was having my usual breakfast of fruit and cheese, when I was struck by the deliciousness of it all. I looked at the label on the cheese. It read:"Expresso/Lavender Rubbed." Then and there, my whole being was transported through the heavens to Sénanque, where I could smell and taste the heavenly lavender. All of a sudden, I awoke with a start, and the cheese/lavender was no less real. Now, my breakfast was prescribed, till it was broken by delicious Chimay beer-rubbed cheese...but that's another story.

OUR LADY OF GETHSEMANI

O ur Lady of Gethsemani is a Trappist abbey founded in Kentucky in 1848, considered the mother house of all Trappists in the United States. I visited this abbey several times in the 1950s, and was always edified by my stays there. On my first visit there, I took a photo of a wall painting depicting various Trappist Luminaries, with de Rance on the bottom right. Naturally, he is represented with the famous skull. This photo was kept in my files for years.

Finally, this photo returned to my mind as I was preparing this book. Retrieved, it was no less intriguing than it was fifty years ago, so I sent an email to the monks at the Abbey. I asked why de Rance is often depicted with a skull on his desk. And whose skull was it?

The answer: "It was the traditional stance in those days, to remember death." My correspondent, Brother Luke, likely had never heard of Madame de Montbazon (see *Monk to Bootlegger*), and if he had read about her, he certainly must have conveniently forgotten.

Thomas Merton, O.C.S.O.

On that first trip to Gethsemani, I had the good fortune to meet Thomas Merton, whom everyone visiting there was scrambling to see. He was a world-renowned spiritual writer, and a thorn in his abbot's crown. He was constantly looking over the abbey wall, wanting to start other Trappist monasteries in South America and elsewhere. Still, he was under the vow of stability, having promised never to leave Gethsemani unless ordered to do so by his superiors. Although his writings placed him in contact with writers all over the world, he fretted his entire monastic life on whether he should leave Gethsemani and become a hermit. So there were many facets to his life and his world. As a famous writer, he exercised special privileges unheard of and unwritten in the Rule.

THOMAS MERTON

(1915-1966)

Merton was born in Prades, French Pyrenes, in 1915 during World War I. When he was several months old, the family left France for the United States and settled in Flushing, New York, where his mother died of cancer in late 1921. The following year, Merton and his father traveled to Bermuda where the father fell in love with American novelist Evelyn Scott, and lived with her a few short years. Owen Merton was an artist and loved France. When they returned to France in 1926, Thomas, eleven, was enrolled in a boarding school in Montauban.

In the 1980s, when I was traveling in France a great deal, especially in the south doing lots of bootlegging, I was still interested in Merton and was reading several of his books. Since Prades was on one of my routes, I stopped in that village twice for lunch. Although there is a small plaque honoring the place where Merton was born, none of the local Frenchmen I met back then remembered him.

After his schooling in England and the United States, Merton became a Trappist monk in Gethsemani, Kentucky, and was ordained in 1949. Already a published poet, he had gained fame when he published *The Seven Storey Mountain* in 1948. People flocked to Gethsemani to see the Holy Man of the Mountain. I am as curious as anyone, so I went down to see him (for a second time), under the guise of a retreat. Sure, I saw him. I was in the choir loft, and I watched for him until all the monks came in. The evening Office started, and no Merton. When he finally came in, I recognized him. I had the urge to shout, "Hi, Tom, you're late!" but as he must have been writing a new book, I overlooked that.

But the band played on.

• • •

Merton generated so much revenue for Gethsemani, I feel he was given special privileges. He received more visitors than the Rule allowed. And he would take walks in the woods with his visitors, always under the guise of "business"—spiritual book writing. He reached such a point of holiness that Father Abbot allowed him to live in a hermitage in the woods indefinitely.

Hermitage

But, woe! He did not die in the arms of our Lord, not yet! It has been written in some books coming out of Gethsemani, that Father Louis (Merton's religious name) was receiving guests there, men and women, day and night, and sometimes they stayed till the wee hours of the morning. I suppose they were all writers, discussing their new books.

A Kentucky bourbon distillery just happened to be their neighbor, and the distillery's truck was seen going through the back roads of the monks property, stopping at the hermitage, delivering several boxes of Bourbon. Why? Men and women love to relax. It was perfectly normal, since they were all writing religious papers, and Merton never took a vow of abstinence.

After a while, the Abbot got a whiff of what was going on and removed the hermitage privilege. Poor Tom Merton, now he would have to go back to being a simple monk.

THOMAS MERTON'S DEATH

In 1968, Merton went to an interfaith conference between Catholic and non-Christian monks in suburban Bangkok, Thailand. After speaking at the conference, it is generally concluded that while stepping out of his bath, he was accidentally electrocuted by an electric fan. Some spread rumors that the last moments of his life were in the presence of a statue of the Buddha. Others said that he was assassinated like Martin Luther King had been.

I believe God struck him down for having broken his Vows of Poverty and Stability.

His body was flown back to the United States on board a U.S. military aircraft returning from Vietnam and was buried in the Gethsemani cemetery.

• • •

While still a monk, and manager of Resurrection Cemetery in Oklahoma City, I made a two-day trip to Gethsemani. Like a cat, I was simply curious. In the monk's cemetery, each grave is marked by a simple metal cross with the name of the deceased and year of birth and year of death. However Merton's grave was nowhere to be found within the cemetery enclosure.

There were other burials in a small area next to the cemetery. That's where I found Thomas Merton's grave. It is my opinion that he had infringed on the Trappist Rule so often, he was not deemed worthy of being buried within the cemetery enclosure, and therefore was buried outside the gates, an old tradition in the Catholic Church. I have perused hundreds of periodicals dealing with his burial, but none has explained this fact.

The guest master told me the old enclosed cemetery is full, and that's the reason Merton is buried outside the enclosure. Believe me, he could not tell a lie with a straight face. I did not believe him for an instant. Returning immediately to the cemetery with my mind trained in cemetery work, it was clear to me that my assumptions were correct. There were still five or six unused graves within the enclosure. How did I know? My trained eyes told me so, and besides, Merton was buried in 1968, and yet I saw dates there subsequent to Merton's death. Trappist monks do not buy cemetery graves pre-need. Everyone is buried in order of death. R.I.P.

The grave of Thomas Merton

ALBUQUERQUE

In my teens and twenties, my modus operandi seems to have been to spend an average of only two years in any one location. That's a lot of shifting, but a benefit of old age is that I can look back on those years as invaluable to my later endeavors. We are always products of our past.

In 1953, I purchased a brand new Studebaker sedan which I kept until 1975, when I junked it with 200,000 miles. After the Cistercian experience, I had reluctantly concluded that God wanted me in a more active community. I made a quick survey of religious communities in the United States, visited my pastor, prayed a lot, and headed for Albuquerque, New Mexico, to the newly formed Little Brothers of the Good Shepherd. I was going from one extreme to the other—the brothers operated a large soup kitchen one block away from the bus and train depot in downtown Albuquerque.

I introduced myself to Brother Mathias and he immediately spotted my accent and recognized my French-Canadian name. He answered, "Nice to meet you," in French. Born in Ireland, he had studied in France as a young man with religious brothers dedicated to nursing the sick. While in his early twenties, that community had sent him to Canada with a Frenchman and an Irishman to open a new house for their order.

Their new hospital in Montreal soon became one of the busiest in Canada. He was successful there, but Mathias' real interest lay with the poor and downtrodden. After ten years in Montreal, he packed his bags and, penniless, hitchhiked his way to San Diego, where he opened a soup kitchen for the poor. After that he ended up opening a soup kitchen in Albuquerque. He later told me he had seen Archbishop Byrnes in Santa Fe and begged for permission to open the soup kitchen. The archbishop saw it as a bottomless pit, and exhausted by Mathias' pleadings, said "No! No! No! Leave me alone, and go in peace." Ah! The Archbishop had said "Go in peace," so Mathias went to Albuquerque and promptly opened his soup kitchen. Such are the makings of a saint and founder of a religious community.

His greeting to me in French surprised me, but his conversation practically knocked me down. Here was an Irishman by birth, speaking French-Canadian with an Irish brogue and an American accent. For the two years I was there, even the brothers at the dinner table had a hard time understanding him, and afterward would ask me, "What did he say?" No wonder there was a turnover of candidates, just as there was later in my own community.

In my initial meeting with Brother Mathias, he spotted my brand new Studebaker behind me. "Ah!" he said. "God has sent you here this very minute. We lost our car only this morning; we need another one, and here it is! God always provides!"

I explained to him I was on the rebound from the Cistercians, had not even finished my Novitiate, and had fallen sick, and now I felt God was calling me to a more active life.

Without missing a beat, Mathias began addressing me as "Brother." "Brother who?" I asked. "You, of course, you are now a Brother of the Good Shepherd." We were still standing in his doorway while a line of homeless men watched us with curious expressions.

"You are now the extant brother. You will use your car to fetch provisions every morning. You do not want these homeless men to go hungry, do you?"

"No, b-b-but..."

"No ifs or buts. We need coffee within the hour. Go to St. Joseph's Hospital, drive around to the back and you will find the cafeteria in the basement. Ask for Sister Joachum and she will give you our coffee for the day. Go in peace."

"But—but my suitcase is still in the car..."

"It's okay, you will manage. In the meantime, I will prepare a room for you. When you return with the coffee, bring in your suitcase and we will show you to your room."

I found the hospital and asked for Sister Joachum. "You're the new brother at the Good Shepherd! Brother Mathias called me and asked me to look for you. You look very kind!" I was already getting into my part.

Every cafeteria has a coffee urn, with the coffee grounds in the top position of the shiny sparkling urn. There were two large empty coffee cans on the counter. She had obviously made coffee with those grounds in early morning and now she was transferring those used grounds back to their original coffee cans, which she presented to me.

"What are these for?" I asked.

"Take these to Brother Mathias."

"No, there must be some mistake. He asked me to get coffee grounds for the shelter! These are already used!"

"Ah, my poor man. This is exactly what they use at the shelter and also for the brothers." From her smile and good natured mien, I took leave. "See ya in the morning, Brother!"

Matthias gave me a room next to his and immediately made me his first assistant. I protested I had no background, but he retorted that I could understand him better than the other brothers (I had known him less than two hours, and had not yet met the others), and besides, I would be his novice master someday. Typical Saint Mathias! I ask a question, he fires back with a bombshell.

My daily morning run consisted of visiting the loading docks of several specific grocery stores. These grocery stores had a lenient policy of leaving their culls of unsaleable fruit and vegetables on the loading docks for farmers or pork producers to pick up, or the following morning it would go in the garbage truck. If I came by at the right time, I had the pick of the crop. Brother Mathias himself personally cleaned all food and made the best tasting nutritional soup I have ever tasted. Three times a day, long lines of hungry and homeless men lined up to eat this soup.

There were five brothers at the refuge when I was there. Brothers were on duty twenty-four hours a day, dispensing food, clothes, and even medical service. Several doctors provided their services at no cost to "the knights of the road," and my job, of course, was to drive the clients to the doctor—in my shiny new Studebaker.

The refuge had two dormitories for men and the only requirement was that guests had to shower and put on clean clothes immediately after registering for the night. One brother manned the front welcome desk—and I manned it often, especially in the evening—and another brother manned the laundry, which was sometimes in use twenty-four hours a day for guests' clothes and brothers' clothes. Two brothers stood duty all night long: one near the front desk as night watchman, and one overseeing the laundry and dormitory. It was a lot of hard work and long hours for only five or six brothers.

Brother Mathias was no slouch himself. He usually manned the kitchen by himself all day with its huge soup pots, and wrote letters all night. I served the soup to the guests each noon and evening.

One day Brother Mathias told me, "We need a novitiate, and I have an idea! Trappists have been in Pecos, New Mexico, for a few years but have found the soil unsuitable for their agrarian life, so they moved farther west. I hear their property is for sale. It would make a nice novitiate for us. Why don't you take a drive out there and find out what you can." With that, he slammed two sandwiches in my hand and sent me on my way.

The property was for sale all right, with a Realtor sign by the road. I jumped over the fence and looked at the buildings. The few sheds that were unlocked were clean and well maintained. I copied the information from the sign, ate my sandwiches, and returned to the Good Shepherd refuge.

The very next afternoon, Brother Mathias and I drove up to Santa Fe to see the Archbishop and explore the possibilities. The Realtors already had a good prospective buyer. Archbishop Byrnes thought Mathias was biting off more than he could chew, so later on, it was the Olivetan Benedictines who purchased the property. Although most Benedictines wear black habits, these are the "white Benedictines" originally from Monte Oliveto, Italy.

Brother Mathias was always optimistic and a visionary. Two months after the Pecos affair, he sent me to look at a property on 12th Street in Albuquerque. He thought it had been owned by a Catholic doctor. It was very large and suitable for a novitiate. From my inquiries, I learned the archdiocese had a mortgage on it. Again, the very next day, we were off to Santa Fe. This time, the entire demarche eventually came to fruition. Archbishop Byrnes even suggested I should be the first Novice Master of the Order. Little did he know I had already given my notice that I would be leaving soon. I was going on to another chapter in my life.

During my two years in Albuquerque, I counseled with priests weekly. Each week's priest gave me a spiritual conference and I got to know them all well. Father Antonin Dumont had been a classmate of my father at the orphanage in Lewiston, Maine, when they were from five to fourteen years old. When he first met me, he recognized me immediately, as I both looked and spoke like my father.

Thirty years after that first meeting, while visiting my father in a hospice in Lewiston, I was surprised to see Father Dumont walking down the hall! He was a fellow patient there and, although ambulatory, clearly had much dementia. He claimed he recognized me, though I wasn't convinced. He died shortly afterward, as did my father.

SERVANTS OF THE HOLY PARACLETE

Father Gerald Fitzgerald

My duties at the Good Shepherd Refuge in Albuquerque required at least one trip weekly to Via Coeli in Jemez Springs, the home of The Servants of the Paraclete, a religious order dedicated to priestly problems, and founded by the Reverend Gerald Fitzgerald from Massachusetts. In the early years of World War II he had served in the active Army, had seen its erosive influence on priests, and founded a new community to meet a real need. Because he paid for my gas and car expenses, I spoke with him on each trip, at least once a week.

In a sense, I was a taxi driver and my fares were mostly drunken priests who had been sent to Via Coeli by their bishops to mend their ways. This was the early 1950s and air travel was not yet entrenched as it is today. They arrived mostly by train or bus, and both stations were together in downtown Albuquerque. Sometimes, but not always, the priests were dressed in black with a Roman collar. But how was I to recognize my fare? I would take the top off a cardboard box and write his last name in large letters. It worked every time, except for once: My priest was dressed in normal, secular clothes and was under the influence. When he saw the card, he avoided me, and headed for the bars.

At my wits' end to locate him, I resorted to contacting the Albuquerque Police Department. Within two hours, he was found in a downtown tavern. He was somewhat belligerent, but was placed in my car by the police. He had a small flask in his back pocket, still half full of booze. They gave it to me, and I placed it in the trunk of the car, and locked it.

The trip to Via Coeli usually took me one and a half hours over desert landscape, and I wasn't going to a picnic. By the time I found my fare, it was already evening and these roads are strange in pitch darkness. New Mexico has open range laws, and since this was Pueblo Indian country, sheep, cattle, and horses roamed freely over the highways at night.

Via Coeli

This priest was in constant chatter, looking for another drink, but I ignored him. Finally, about halfway home, while I was driving seventy miles per hour, my fare placed his arm around my neck and tried to strangle me. I was seeing stars and was afraid he would succeed. I applied the brakes as quickly as I could and he went careening all over the back seat. When the car stopped, I jumped out quickly, opened the back door, grabbed him, and gave him an uppercut on the chin. He was quiet the remainder of the trip.

Arriving in Via Coeli, I went in haste to see Father Fitzgerald, and in a confessional mode, I accused myself of having "hit" a priest. "I am sorry you had to resort to that, Brother, but I suppose you had to do what you had to do. With my blessing, go in peace." With that, he doubled my stipend for that trip.

Prior to founding the Paracletes, Father Fitzgerald had never considered priests as child abusers. He told me once, "We never had any instruction on child abuse in the seminary. It was as if it was nonexistent. Following our education, we would have treated it as a mortal sin." The Catholic Church never understood the damage which child abuse does to the child. The minute this oversight became evident to Father Fitzgerald, he acquired an island in the Caribbean with the explicit purpose of sequestering the child-abuser priests there. When he went to Rome to present his plan to the Pope, Rome understood the problem much less than he did, and instead considered only the unwanted publicity it would engender.

Priest child abusers created very bad press for Father Fitzgerald. Twenty-first century writers have not been kind to him, but it is still my firm opinion that Father Fitzgerald was a saintly man. His community spread over to Europe, and now they have a Generalate in Rome.

Stationed at Via Coeli was another classmate of my father, Reverend Emilien Faucher, the organist. When I had walked 300 miles on snowshoes to Montreal, he had followed the trek daily in the newspaper. Five years later, when I first met him, no introduction was needed. When I knocked on his door, he took one look at me, blurted out my name, and gave me a big embrazo.

HERMANOS FOSSORES DE LA MISERICORDIA

"GRAVEDIGGING BROTHERS OF MERCY"

That title well fits The Brothers of St. Joseph, but it is the name of another community in Spain, which was founded in the early 1950s. At that time I had written them for information, and the founder wrote me back in Spanish about his ideals, and what life was like in a Campo Santo in Guadix, Spain. Their entire structure coincided with my ideals. I inquired, if I entered their monastery and remained for ten years, whether they would entertain the possibility of sending me back to the United States to start a branch of their community.

What a bombshell!

Apparently, no way, Jose! The founder wrote that no one bargains for entrance into a community, nor into the thereafter. Point final. They sure had the Campo Santo frame of mind, so I directed my thought to other endeavors. However, they remained in the abysmal recesses of my mind, and I would think of them again later.

A short-lived pictorial magazine of the 1950s for American Catholics was *Jubilee*. Its founders were Thomas Merton (a Trappist), Robert Lax, and Ed Rice. I had met Merton at the Trappist Abbey in Gethsemani, Kentucky, in the 1950s. (Today, I buy their fruitcakes and cheeses online for the holidays.) Merton suggested *Jubilee* send a photographer to Lafayette,

Louisiana, where I spent two years learning cemetery work. The end result was an interesting article entitled "Brothers of the Dead," printed in the magazine with fitting photos of The Brothers of St. Joseph in the Louisiana cemetery. Many letters were received as a result of this article. Archbishop Cody of New Orleans sent us a letter of congratulations. Bishop Reed of Oklahoma invited us to come settle in Oklahoma City. The Holy Spirit works in mysterious ways. In 1970, I received letters from three separate Spanish Hermanos requesting admittance into The Brothers of St. Joseph, with some stipulations. I reminded them that nobody, but nobody, ever bargains for admittance into religious communities.

In the 1980s, while on a bootlegging trip to France, I detoured through Spain to visit my previous correspondents, the Hermanos Fossores in Guadix. Arriving in town in late afternoon, I was too chicken and too spoiled by modern conveniences to go to their monastery that night, so I rented a motel room in town. In the morning, I presented myself to the Hermanos, and they welcomed me with a big embrazo. I spent the day visiting and chatting with them, then rode off into the sunset.

The Guadix Hermanos

PENITENTES

Lummis's photo of a Penitente crucifixion ritual near San Mateo, New Mexico, 1888
Courtesy of the Southwest Museum, Los Angeles

Rev. John Sigstein was the original founder of the Victory Noll sisters, which had 300 members. Later Sigstein became a retired hermit in Tijeras Canyon, east of Albuquerque, and as he was in poor health, I did his grocery shopping each week. I also drove him down to the Brothers of the Good Shepherd for his weekly conference, and then returned him home. He could hardly live alone in his hermitage. I volunteered to stay with him to see to his needs, a blessed three months for me indeed.

On one of his better days, I accompanied him on a visit to a Penitente Morada, where he gave a conference. Ah! I was thrilled and here's why.

When I was in my teens at Saint Dominic High School in Maine, I had to submit an essay on the Penitentes. It was Holy Week and the local newspapers had run stories about one of the Penitentes' members who had been crucified alive on a wood cross, and kept exposed there for three hours, and then taken down as our Lord had been 2000 years ago. It was a devotion of the Penitentes. I received an A for my essay. Now, ten years later, here I was among them.

The Penitentes were a secret brotherhood of Hispanics in New Mexico and southern Colorado in the 1800s and early 1900s. They practiced flagellation, possibly influenced by flagellants of Spain and Italy a thousand years before. It is not necessarily a new devotional practice, yet some religious orders still practice it today, including Cistercians, who have done so since their inception. But the Penitentes had gone further.

During Holy Week, in devotion to the passion of Christ, a member in many moradas would be crucified and hanged from a cross for three hours, then brought down and nursed back to health.

The flagellants were excommunicated in the fourteenth century. Eventually the flagellants were absorbed into other communities and some of their practices—such as giving oneself physical discipline—still remain today in some monasteries.

In the latter part of the nineteenth century, the Penitentes were excommunicated, but in January 1947, Archbishop Byrnes of New Mexico officially recognized the Penitentes as an organization, thus lifting the excommunication. Actually, it was Father John Sigstein who brought them back into the church, even though Archbishop Byrnes received the credit for it.

History repeats itself.

MONSIGNOR FINN

© *To Bury the Dead*

Monsignor Finn was the rector of St. Francis de Sales Seminary in northwest Oklahoma City. He was the first rector, and for all practical purposes, the only rector. I write as such, because he was transferred to the Cathedral in Tulsa, and another priest teacher, Father Donovan, was named to replace him as rector. It was a long time ago, and my memory fails me at times. It was early summer, probably as the seminarians were going home for the summer vacations. Father Donovan was named to replace him, and the diocese suddenly decided to close the seminary in later summer. So Father Donavan may not have been rector when seminarians were present.

From the beginning, my relations with Monsignor Finn and the staff at the seminary were proper and cool. I've always believed in minding my own business. I did not even go and introduce myself, for there was no reason to do so. I lived in Bethany for seven years and, at the time, I had no business being close to the property. Monsignor Finn and the staff thought the brothers were just a flash in the pan, and would peter out in a few months. I was perfectly at ease with this entente.

A few months later, the diocese hired a cemetery architect, resulting in a contract for a turnkey project: earth-moving, land-contouring, road-carving, and map-platting. It ended there.

I visited the property several times with Bishop Reed, but we never went to the seminary. After that I went many times by myself just to look at the fields and vales, dreaming, and making plans in my mind. At that point, Bishop Reed placed the entire project in my hands. The diocese was paying for everything, so I cleared everything with the bishop before going ahead.

As soon as the first piece of earth-moving equipment was delivered to the property, I went to the property daily, until I officially took working possession of the future cemetery. In the meantime, I split my time and energy between the cemetery and developing the Brothers of St. Joseph.

I purchased a backhoe to work the land and later to open graves, along with other equipment. We needed space for this equipment, so Bishop Reed arranged with Monsignor Finn that the cemetery and brothers would share the seminary garage and workshop with them. Monsignor Quinn was cool to the request, but since it was requested by the bishop and you never say no to a bishop, he acquiesced. I received proof of his state of mind and it confirmed my suspicions.

I do not remember the first time I met Monsignor Finn; it is lost in the labyrinth of my old mind. But he remained cool for the first three years the seminary was opened, and it stayed that way until he needed a favor from me, several years later—in the Robert affair.

In our second year in Oklahoma, we received an inquiry from a young man from Wisconsin, by the first name of James. We sent him our standard reply: a letter, a pamphlet, and a questionnaire. A month passed before we heard from him again.

Unknown to us, he consulted his pastor regarding our status, and was advised to write the bishop of the diocese, Bishop Reed. When James received a beautiful letter from Bishop Reed (see Brother James story), he wasted no time in completing the questionnaire and asking for admission. The rest is history.

James turned out to be a hell of a gentleman—rarely did we receive the equal to him in our community. He had many talents and always accepted what was asked of him. When he arrived, we needed a cook, and he turned out to be the best cook we ever had, before or since. Some time later, we were asked to furnish two cooks to the orphanage to relieve the nuns of their heavy load. Brother James promptly volunteered, and I named another brother to help him. James commanded the kitchen at St. Joseph's Orphanage efficiently and economically, all the while cooking for twenty-seven brothers, and seeing that the food landed on our tables. How's that for a gentleman?

Things were going too well. The seminary had the same problems as the orphanage. The four nuns working in the seminary kitchen were from the Order of the Precious Blood, of Wichita, Kansas. They were always tired, and it was determined that washing and lifting those cooking pots and pans was contributing to their problems, and extra help was needed. Monsignor Finn did not dare to hire lay people to work in the kitchen with the nuns, because they were semi-cloistered. So why not explore the possibility of having two BSJs helping the nuns? After all, the BSJs are monks . . . and there are twenty-seven of them. Why not query hard-nosed and intractable Joseph and see how he feels?

The very next day, Vic, the cemetery maintenance man, approached me and said, "Monsignor Finn would like to talk to you."

When and where, I asked.

"He's in his office right now!"

"That's fine. If he wants to see me, why doesn't he come to me? Or call me?"

That evening, Monsignor Finn called me at our monastery in Bethany.

He had the voice of an angel, and so friendly. To make a long story short, he was asking what I thought of the idea of loaning him two brothers every day to help the nuns in the kitchen. It hit me like a bombshell! Then I reminded myself that we were in the service of God and humanity, and I must be receptive.

"Yes, we have twenty-seven brothers," I said, "but I keep them all working. Let me sleep on this, and float the idea with the brothers." After all, we were democratic.

That evening, after dinner and before evening prayers, I called all the brothers together to convey the contents of the query, indicating we were here first to serve God in the persons of our fellow human beings.

The air was electric: it was obvious everyone was smug and happy with James as the master cook, and behold, James was the first one to talk:

"I would gladly volunteer if you want me to."

"Well, James, you are indispensible at the orphanage, and overseeing that the brothers do not starve!"

"Brother Joseph, no one is indispensable. What would you do if I dropped dead?"

That was another bombshell—two in one day. I thought I would lose my sanity. I went to the night prayers, then straight to bed to sleep on it.

First thing in the morning, I told James I respected his opinion very much and would go along with him, and would call Monsignor Finn to let him know. But it would be one week before he starts: to give us the time to make necessary arrangements, we would have to find a helper for him at the seminary, find a replacement at the orphanage kitchen, etc.

God always provides to those who do His work. Brother Bill Twomey, another fine gentleman, immediately volunteered, and replaced James at the orphanage without batting an eye, and without missing a cup of coffee.

My biggest problem was in finding a helper for James at the seminary. I had to send someone worthy of the position, who could really be of help to Jim. On the other hand, I could not appoint a brother who was happy working at Resurrection Cemetery, well adjusted, and productive. After sleeping on this problem all night, the spirit pointed to only one man—Robert.

ROBERT

Robert was born in Moline, Illinois, and educated in parochial schools. He was the son of a doting mother and a harsh father. Somewhat chubby, he had never worked a day in his life. The teaching nuns had instilled in him the fear and love of God, and the absolute necessity to organize his life to end up in Heaven. So Robert concluded The Brothers of St. Joseph was the answer.

With the usual correspondence, acceptance, etc., Robert ended with the BSJ in Oklahoma. Lazy and absolutely worthless in the cemetery, he was the natural candidate for James' helper at the seminary. But heaven forbid that I should foist him on James. So I immediately went to see James at the orphanage kitchen.

I took him aside and in a low tone asked him what he thought of the possibility of having Robert as a helper. James did not miss a beat. He smiled. "I am sure he is the best man you can spare. I would be happy to work with Robert."

I immediately turned around so Jim would not see me crying, and headed for the chapel.

When I woke the following morning, I realized I had fallen asleep in the chapel pew. I hurried to our mother house for a quick shower and change of clothes. I was none the worse for it, and the brothers were none the wiser.

Something strange happened that week. The mother house had two stories, and I was the only one whose sleeping room was on the first floor. My room was located next to the refectory and the kitchen. Coming out of my bedroom, on the left was a restroom, and on the right a door to the refectory. But if I stayed in the small hall where our library stood, a door led to the stairway to the second floor.

From the library there was another door with three or four stairs going down to the split-level addition to this building. It was fairly large and had been built during World War II of blood bricks. Even clay or cement bricks were scarce during the war, so a cattleman from the stockyards thought of using animal blood mixed with sand to make bricks. It made for a very sturdy addition to this old, decrepit house.

This addition was used as our recreation room. It contained a television set, an old-time player piano, a card table, three large sofas, and three easy chairs.

Most brothers went directly to the recreation room immediately after dinner, and stayed there till the evening prayer bell was heard. After evening prayers was the Grand Silence and brothers were not allowed in the rec room.

Immediately after night prayers, I went to my room and closed the door. All was quiet on the western front, and I went to sleep immediately.

I was wakened by the sound of music after 10 p.m., an unusual event, so I sat up on the bed to make sure I was *not dreaming*. Sure enough it was real, though ephemeral. In the dark of night and in my underwear, I followed the sound of music down to the recreation room—and there was Robert. Clad only in extra-large pajama bottoms, Robert. Performing the ballet *Swan Lake* with all the motions and emotions of a gala performance, jumping from one sofa to another, and flapping his wings—Robert.

Though it was comical and worth watching, my blood boiled and my emotions ran in high gear.

I simply said, "Robert."

He froze and his mouth fell open; he looked at me, speechless and embarrassed.

"Robert, real men don't dance that way, though you are very good at it. Please go to bed and we will talk tomorrow."

The following morning, I managed to see Robert alone. I congratulated him for his good performance, but pointed out it had been after evening prayers and therefore forbidden. I rarely gave brothers punishment.

"Don't worry, Robert, there won't be any punishment. Actually you may take two days off to rest, and prepare to accompany Brother James to the seminary kitchen next week." His sigh of relief could not hide his elation.

The seminary kitchen faced Resurrection Cemetery, which was adjacent to the seminary. Brother James and Brother Robert left our monastery at 8 AM along with the brothers working at the cemetery. They traveled in the same trucks, which was very convenient for all of us.

James and Robert took to the seminary kitchen like fish to water. They both loved the nuns (being that type), and of course the nuns doted on them. The lovely Monsignor Finn called to tell me how well things worked out that first week. I simply thanked him for his call.

James and Robert worked in the seminary kitchen for two months, both seemingly very happy. The nuns seemed to gravitate toward Robert, and were often seen talking with him.

Then one evening before night prayers, James asked to see me in private. He told me that Robert frequently complained to the nuns that I was a gruesome taskmaster to the brothers working in the cemetery. The nuns had an hour of free time after lunch, and would allow only Brother Robert in their cloistered quarters . . . and Robert would keep them entertained by dancing for them, by jumping from one piece of furniture to another and "performing" Swan Lake and other popular pieces.

When Robert was at the sink washing pots and pans, he would keep an eye out through the window above the sink, and call out to one of the nuns, "Come here, quick! Look who's driving by again! It's Brother Joseph—you never see that guy walking! He's always toodling around in that fancy air-conditioned car, leaving the brothers to slave out in the cemetery." (The fancy air-conditioned car was my old 1953 Studebaker with over 200,000 miles to its credit.)

Brother Jim told me, "I'm not a tattletale, but it has reached the point where it hurts our community, and will damage our relations with the seminary. I can live with it, but I am not the superior!"

Robert had exhausted my confidence. I immediately called him to my office and told him that I was aware of his exotic dancings for the nuns, and his diatribe against the slave driver. I told him to pack his clothes so I could personally drive him to the airport.

I drove Robert to the airport in silence, without incident. At the last moment I suggested he pick up his life where he had left off, and that he would be much the better for it.

Bon voyage, Robert!

I returned to the cemetery to take up where I had left off.

James had selected a replacement in the person of Brother George, who would be a perfect fit. Born and educated in Oklahoma City, he was also a darling to the nuns.

However, despite my safe delivery of Robert to the airport, unknown to me, a new, strange Robert odyssey had begun.

Later I learned that as soon as I left the airport and headed back to Resurrection Cemetery, Robert hailed a taxi and headed for downtown Oklahoma City. After renting a room in a flophouse, he called the seminary kitchen. When a nun answered, he told her about his predicament, and that he was heartbroken to leave the nuns and their seminary kitchen. The nun requested his address, told him to stay put, and promised to contact him soon.

Of course, I was unaware of these shenanigans, but it all came out in the wash. One of our brothers was working at St. Anthony Hospital, and was downtown on an errand for his superiors. While stopped at a red light, he noticed two nuns stopping their car at an old flophouse. When the nuns actually went inside, he raised an eyebrow.

That night at dinnertime I was the recipient of his report. Perplexed, I decided I'd better keep my own eyes and ears open.

The following morning, as I went to the seminary garage to take the backhoe, maintenance man Vic approached me.

"Brother Joseph, Robert spent the night here at the seminary, and plans to start work here in the kitchen at noon."

What? Hadn't I dropped him at the airport the previous day?

"Vic, that's impossible!" I said.

He looked serious. "Believe me, I talked with him last night for fifteen minutes, and he spent much time with Monsignor Finn."

Now everything gelled in my mind. I picked up the phone.

"Monsignor Finn, I understand Robert spent the night at the seminary last night."

"Why, uh, no—I haven't seen Robert for two days."

"Are you sure of that?"

"Why should I lie to you?"

"Okay, okay, Monsignor Finn." I lost some of my steam. "Thank you for the information." Click.

It made no sense. After stewing a while, I decided to walk over to the seminary and just show up at Monsignor Finn's office.

When he saw me charge into his office like a bull in a china closet, Monsignor Finn turned white. I told him I had incontrovertible proof that Robert had found his way back to the seminary the night before—witnesses who saw and talked to Robert told me so. Monsignor Finn looked me straight in the eye *and denied everything*!

Steam came out of my ears. "Brother James and Brother George are being removed from the seminary this very moment, and if you ever see a Brother of St. Joseph in this seminary again, it will be over my dead body!"

Imagine the gall of a Monsignor of the Catholic church lying to your face!

I picked up Brothers James and George and headed back home to the mother house in Bethany.

CHAPTER 3

THE BROTHERS

LAFAYETTE

The basic reason the pastor wanted brothers in Lafayette is that in the past, Calvary Cemetery had a lot of burials in the wrong lots. The records had not been corrected, and it was time to make an entirely new set of records. Calvary was a beautiful Louisiana cemetery, with large magnolia trees, and huge oak trees draped in hanging moss. The cemetery had several burial sections, each with different-sized lots. It was an anagram, and I was to sort it out. Louisiana has a high water table, and the vaults were buried halfway in the ground with the lids exposed and whitewashed. Each fall before All Souls Day, lot owners would come to the cemetery and whitewash their own vault and their relatives' vaults, and sometimes even those of deceased lot owners who had no interested survivors.

My relationship to the pastor or the bishop had never been defined and was ambiguous at best. I was not planning on being at Calvary the rest of my life, but I desired to learn all I could about cemeteries and leave the rest to the Lord and Divine Providence.

I was soon joined by Ed, a white-haired old man with stooped shoulders, who was unable to work in the cemetery except to arrange flowers in fallen vases, or rake a few leaves. He became the cook and chief bottle washer.

Whether I was alone or with ten other brothers, I had determined to live according to the Rule of Saint Benedict—that I would live by the labor of my hands. My specific verbal arrangement with the pastor was that all our needs would be met. From the very first, the pastor brought us several bags of groceries, and did so every week without the benefit of a list. We took what was given—what God had provided. There were two people already working in the cemetery, a black man by the name of Kelley, and his twenty-year-old son. They dug graves by hand, mowed grass, and did odd jobs. As manager I decided to keep the Kelleys on the payroll. Yet I was not on the payroll, for the Brothers of Saint Joseph had only a verbal agreement that Father Fortier would provide living expenses. Would I ever do that today?

Hell, no!

I never saw a one dollar bill coming into my hands from Father Fortier.

Several months later, on a cold January day, the Kelleys showed up without their customary lunch bag. They worked hard all morning and at noon went to the work shed but didn't show any signs of eating their customary lunches. It turned out they were in the process of moving from one house to another, and Kelley's wife had not prepared any lunches.

It was a penetratingly cold day, and I said to them, "No way! Come and have warm soup with us."

"No, no, Brother, we can't do that."

"Why not?"

"No, no, we can't."

I insisted, and almost had to drag them physically to my abode—a house trailer. Finally we were installed at the kitchen table, and old brother Ed served us a delicious hot soup. While eating, we heard noises outdoors. It was the pastor and the chairman of the cemetery board. They each had a grocery bag in their arms. The minute the father and son at our table saw Father Fortier, they bolted for the door and ran away. The pastor and his companion promptly put the two grocery bags back in the car, and later came in to talk to me.

"Didn't you know that in this part of the country white men and black men don't socialize, much less eat at the same table? If we ever see you break deep south customs again, we're going to tar and feather you and run you out of town."

Brother Ed and I stayed for another year, but never saw another grocery bag from the pastor. Still, we managed to survive. Father Fortier's sister-in-law, Juanita Fortier, furnished us grocery bags full of food, sometimes from Father Fortier's own pantry.

God does provide.

Yet, later, the pastor had the audacity one day to tell me, "Within two or three years, I should be able to make over one million dollars with you here!"

I had the opportunity to learn all phases of cemetery work: how to design new cemeteries, plat new sections, make burial transfers, and work with concrete and pour concrete vaults.

The pastor insisted I go to Martin & Castille Funeral Home and tell the owner that we also would be selling burial vaults. At first, I refused.

In fairness to funeral directors, I must point out their overhead: large funeral homes must be cooled in summer and heated in winter, have someone on duty twenty-four hours a day, maintain a freezer, an embalming room, viewing rooms, chapels, hearses, limousines—

oftentimes without a funeral to arrange for days or weeks. They absolutely need to make some profit on every aspect of their services.

After repeated entreaties, I reluctantly agreed to visit the funeral director Paul Castille. Martin & Castille had a beautiful funeral home, with a long front porch in the Louisiana tradition. On that porch I met Paul Castille and spilled the beans. As manager of Calvary Cemetery, I told Paul, "I'm here to inform you that from now on, I will sell the vaults, and my cemetery crew will install them."

Being new to cemetery work, and still green behind the ears, I did not understand all the ramifications. I thought I had done my duty by Father Fortier and God. Yet I learned that for Paul it was a thunderclap.

"You son of a bitch!" He stood up. "If you think you're going to come here and defile my beautiful funeral home and tell me how to run my business, I'll kill you!" He started toward me! Realizing the situation, I pivoted on one foot and ran out to my car, speeding away as fast as I could. That was in 1958. Since then, I've never presumed to tell a funeral director what to do.

• • •

Jubilee, a new pictorial magazine of that time, published a picture story, "Brothers of the Dead." It must have been 1958 or 1959. The pictures were very striking, showing the white-haired, stoop-shouldered Brother Ed working with me around graves under a huge oak tree with hanging moss. This story brought in many letters from all over the country, most from prospective members of The Brothers of St. Joseph, and three from bishops inquiring about the possibility of us working in their diocese.

Newly named Bishop Victor J. Reed of the diocese of Oklahoma City/Tulsa was one of the inquirers. That was the offer we could not refuse. It was not a question of money or compensation because at no time did we seek more than our barest subsistence. But once again, Divine Providence had provided.

THE BROTHERS IN OKLAHOMA

© *To Bury the Dead*

© *To Bury the Dead*

FRANCIS

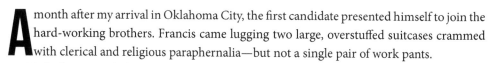

A month after my arrival in Oklahoma City, the first candidate presented himself to join the hard-working brothers. Francis came lugging two large, overstuffed suitcases crammed with clerical and religious paraphernalia—but not a single pair of work pants.

He had previously been with a community of teaching brothers and never ceased telling me how happy he had been there, but Francis said God was calling him to the Brothers of Saint Joseph. We spent several long evenings discussing my vision for the BSJ, such as my own happiness with the Cistercians in Canada seven years previous. I was hoping to emulate their spirit in the observance of the Rule of Saint Benedict, which encouraged silence as much as possible, within reason.

Francis had a good laugh at my expense. "American boys will never accept your spirit, Joe." He was right, and I never succeeded in conveying that spirit to my future confrères.

The following morning, I told Francis, "We are going to town to buy you a pair of dungarees." While the new brother Francis expressed happiness at having work clothes, I would soon see that he usually found an excuse not to have to wear those coveted trousers.

A few weeks later, I absented myself to check on the work in progress at our new Resurrection Cemetery. Upon returning to our quarters, guess what I saw promenading in our large parking lot. It was Francis reciting his breviary, but sporting an ornate clerical outfit with a Roman collar, a cape and a biretta—at least four layers of clothes in ninety-six-degree August heat.

The biretta went out of style at least a century previous, along with the cape. The Brothers of Saint Joseph never wore a Roman collar, which was usually reserved for clerics. Our religious habit was a simple black cassock held together by a leather belt, as specified in the Rule of Saint Benedict. Francis was as averse to leather belts as he was to work.

Standing in the parking lot, I got the picture immediately, but was too timid to dismiss him. With great effort I restrained myself and asked God for the courage to show humility and kindness. I asked Francis to go to his quarters to remove his costume, and come back for a discussion.

This pause provided me time to compose myself, and think about the coming discussion. I recalled that in the entire month he had been here, he had never worn the dungarees I had purchased for him, and had not worked a single day.

When Francis returned, I suggested he had come to the Brothers of Saint Joseph by mistake. Before I could go further, he interrupted me:

"Yes, I know. I realize that now, but I have found a priest in Oklahoma who will employ me as an elementary school teacher!"

"For heaven's sake, Francis, grab it, and God bless you!"

The following morning, Father Richard Dolan was at my door and they left happily. As they were leaving for the 133-mile trip, I prayed a common phrase seen in cemeteries, that they would be happy forever.

The week after school started in September, much to my surprise I saw Father Richard and Francis pulling up in my driveway. Father got out first and declared he was bringing Francis "back home," because this is where he had picked him up. He had brought Francis back because Francis had not followed the pastor's guidelines for those who live close to the elementary school. By that time, Francis had gotten out of the car, and jovially declared, like the prodigal son, "I've come back home!"

"Well, Father Richard, you knew full well the circumstances under which you hired Francis. And, Francis, what I said to Father Richard also goes for you. Now, both of you get back in that car, and get the hell out."

They skiddoed in a powder.

Three hours later, Bishop Reed called me: "Brother Joseph, Francis is here with a Carmelite father from whom he had gone begging money for his fare home. It seems you enticed him to come to Oklahoma, but would not pay his fare back home." The statement sounded like boolsheet to me. *Please, God, do not let Bishop Reed become embroiled in this maelstrom.*

"Bishop Reed, the facts are not exactly as you purported, but it's immaterial. When I came to Oklahoma City, we signed an entente agreement, you and I. You guaranteed full autonomy for The Brothers of St. Joseph. And now, I beg you to respect our full autonomy."

Bishop Reed gently placed the phone down, and that's the last I saw or heard of Francis.

• • •

Whew! I'm so glad it's over. This story has given me more headaches than any other in *Monk to Bootlegger*. I can't believe I've tackled it again in this book.

A few years later, I read in a Catholic newspaper that Francis had formed a new religious community in Illinois, across the river from St. Louis, and were called Franciscan Brothers of Christ the King.

From that day on, I followed Francis's career on the web. Oh my! A career fit for a fallen angel! Dear reader, if you are intrigued, make a computer search on those Brothers, or Francis Skube.

304

BROTHER JOHN

In December 1960, John was the first visitor and prospective member to visit The Brothers of St. Joseph in Bethany, Oklahoma. He lived in Lexington, Oklahoma, about an hour's drive from our residence. He seemed pleased with our environment, and never batted an eye. We discussed his possible entry into The Brothers of St. Joseph, and he agreed to return after the holidays, early in January.

Having been born on a farm, John anticipated gaining experience from his new venture with The Brothers of St. Joseph. Soon he was joined by two other new members, and together they formed a triumvirate of the best three working brothers any community could have, bar none.

After a year, John approached me. "This work is similar to the farm work I've been doing ever since I can remember. I greatly love this community, but I also would love to be an X-ray technician. I really can't decide. My favorite aunt lives alone in Colorado Springs. She would love to have me stay with her, and she would pay for my education. Can you help me decide what to do?"

I will never stand in the way of anyone wishing to improve himself. We discussed the pros and cons over several days, the result being that John went on to Colorado Springs at his own expense, trusting that he would not lose his seniority in The Brothers of St. Joseph. We were to discuss his future endeavors when he returned to Oklahoma City. We both trusted each other's suggestions and decisions.

After a year of study in Colorado Springs, John returned to visit us. He still had one more year of study at Mercy Hospital in Oklahoma City. Could he take his old place with the

Brothers?

"Of course, John!" Another year later, John had his credentials, and accepted a position as an isotope technician at St. Antony Hospital in downtown Oklahoma City.

We had twenty-seven members in the community with a monthly income of only $200 to feed them—plus all our other expenses. It was impossible, and we were begging Catholic Charities and St. Joseph's Orphanage for food. When John began receiving a full monthly paycheck at St. Anthony Hospital, that saved the day. God always provides.

While John's income went for current expenses such as food, clothing, and transportation, the commissions I made selling lots for Resurrection Cemetery in my so-called spare time went to a special account for medical and insurance purposes. Now, we were financially stable.

John remained with the brothers as long as they lasted.

After forty years at St. Anthony Hospital, John retired with good Social Security income. After retirement, he could not relax. Always a hard worker, John was always working in the yard around his house, and at friends' houses. When he hears of a sick person, he visits and offers to help. Retired, he probably performs more good deeds than when he was with the brothers. He volunteers four days a week at an animal shelter in Yukon, feeding cats, cleaning cages, and even taking cats out for a walk. He was always a cat lover. I always joke that John works in a cat house. He won't smile when he hears that, but he bears with me. The other three days a week, John is still ready to help other people. Don't you wish we had more like him in this world?

After my exit from Resurrection Cemetery, once my bootlegging had begun in earnest, I told John about my visits to France. I said that if he would like to see France, he could accompany me. He could pay for his trip by helping me carry heavy miniature bottles from my rental car to the Jetport in Paris, then into New York through U.S. Customs, and then to the transfer terminal. Although I made sure he understood the procedure, I failed to mention that his assistance would make him an accomplice in bootlegging. Certain things are better left unsaid!

Three months passed before John availed himself of my offer. Soon we were spending his vacation time in Paris, where it is as cold in February as it in in Oklahoma. As we roamed the busy streets of Paris, I was puzzled to hear "Mercy!" — "Mercy!" — "Mercy!" — "Mercy!" It was John. Since passersby likely didn't know a word of English, I wondered why John was murmuring "Mercy!" to almost everyone he passed.

Finally I realized it was a simple case of mispronunciation. John was trying to offer a grateful "Merci!" every time someone on those narrow French sidewalks stepped aside for us. I had to shake my head and smile: John has always had such a good heart!

BROTHER DON

Don came to The Brothers of St. Joseph at age 18—of Franco-American origins, as I was. It was the end of January 1961, and cold outside, but he was from Michigan, used to cold winters. Along with Brothers John and Norman, he was one of the first real Brothers of St. Joseph in Oklahoma. They formed a triumvirate of the very best working brothers a community could have. These three men spent that first winter working outdoors: balling and burlapping trees, moving two out-of-state cemeteries, and measuring and platting the entire Resurrection Cemetery area. No one ever complained that first winter; they were the epitome of the perfect monks.

Norman and Don platting the cemetery

Then one day, retching his soul and sobbing, Don came to me.

"Brother Joseph, I must go back home. I miss my family so much, I must go back to them." Don was still homesick for his parents, brothers, and sisters, who lived in Michigan.

In many communities in the world, the superiors exercise all types of pressure in such a case; it is a practice as old as Christianity. In the middle ages, some monasteries had their own dungeons and would incarcerate anyone wishing to leave. In modern times, such coercion has given rise to books, movies, videos, and stories, with themes such as, "I leap over the walls," or "I was a prisoner in my own church."

When anyone came to me wishing to leave, I figured he had given the matter ample thought and I never tried to dissuade him. What will be, will be! Let it be.

Don preferred traveling by train and had brought just enough money with him to pay for his return fare home. I have difficulty handling emotional situations, so when I drove him to the old Santa Fe train station, I parked slightly off the entrance, to ease his last contact with the Brothers.

He had taken his two suitcases out of the car and reached the doorway of the train depot, when he dropped the suitcases and ran back to the car sobbing.

"I just want to say one last good-bye!"

I made sure to wait for him to be well into the train station before driving away. I figured there was a fifty-fifty chance that Don would be back. After all, he was still only eighteen.

The first four or five years in Oklahoma, the brothers would place a very small vocational ad in various Catholic publications—our main source of recruits. Brother Don was gone, but not forgotten. That first winter, I had photographed him looking through a surveyor's level, surveying the cemetery. In our ad, the photo was indicative of the work performed by The Brothers of St. Joseph.

It happened that the vocational ad had appeared in diocesan newspapers in Michigan, and one day I got a call. Don was on the line—still bawling.

"Brother Joseph, I'm ready to come back home to Oklahoma, if you will have me back."

Don had a good sense of humor, and at recreation he always was the life of the party. He had a green thumb and loved to work with trees and flowers. We acquired multiflora red rose bushes to be planted at the entrance of Resurrection Cemetery, and he was happiest when working with the roses. Bishop Reed loved the roses as well, and asked Don to plant some at his residence and office in downtown Oklahoma City. Whenever I had to absent myself due to other pressing matters, Don was always the ipso facto leader of the brothers working in the cemetery.

One day, I asked Don to deliver a package to Monsignor Isenbart who was Director of Catholic Charities in this diocese. Catholic Charities had loaned start-up funds for

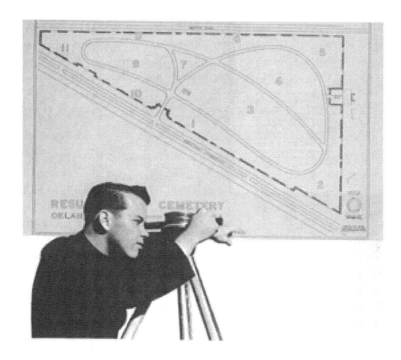

Resurrection Cemetery, and per normal procedure, it was supervising our finances until repayment.

"I will deliver the package, no problem," Don replied, "but I will not call him Monsignor. Do you know what the word means? It means My Lord in English. I will call no man My Lord!" Don's last name was Chabot. In my spare time, I often read old French stories. I smiled in my beard when I read "Le Duel de Jarnac." The Lord of Jarnac was a Chabot.

"But, Don, it's just a title. He's worked hard for that title, and deserves it. By calling him *monsignor*, you are honoring him and acknowledging his achievements."

Don would not be moved. "Granted, he deserves the title, but as an American, I call no man *monsignor!*"

In 1962, Pope John XXIII opened the Vatican Council II, composed of all the bishops in the world, with the explicit purpose of opening the windows of the Catholic Church, and letting the fresh air come in. And it sure did. Religious communities interpreted their rule with a more human touch, and oftentimes reviewed and rewrote their rules and constitutions to be more amenable to the modern world. We were not immune to this fresh air, but I had always held a stricter Cistercian outlook, and it broke my heart to ease our rules.

Now, after his hard work in the cemetery all day, Don wanted the freedom to leave the grounds and roam at will. I trusted him and made a vehicle available to him, providing he return to our residence by curfew time—10 p.m. He never disappointed me in that regard, but the damage to his religious vocation had been done. Eventually he decided to leave the community, but not Oklahoma. His ten years with The Brothers of St. Joseph had weaned him from Michigan. At that time, anyone leaving the brothers after ten years, would be given an automobile, and a portion of the brothers' savings to enable him to get settled again.

The first day on his own, Don found a job in a large apartment complex. He received weekly pay for taking care of the shrubbery, plus an apartment of his own. A year later, he acquired his own home in north Oklahoma City, and operated his own landscape business until his retirement.

When The Brothers of St. Joseph came to an end in 1974, Don received the surveyor's level which had played such a role in his vocation.

BROTHER NORMAN

Norman came from Florida. He had married at eighteen but divorced ten years later, and on the rebound he chose to come to The Brothers of St. Joseph. Quiet and unassuming, he was the exact opposite of Brother Don, who spoke constantly and coined jokes faster than the United States Mint. Norman was the quintessential monk. Everyone followed Don for his humor and humanity, and followed Norman for his holiness. He knew how to do anything and everything in the cemetery. He was numero uno on the indispensable triumvirate, along with Brothers John and Don.

I have been searching my brain to find a funny, enjoyable, or even negative event about Brother Norman, but come up with a complete blank—proof of how unassuming he was. Without batting an eye, Norman would fit perfectly in a strict cloistered order of monks. Six years later, he came to me to say he was leaving for good the following morning. I never asked him why, though we looked at each other with tears in our eyes.

We never heard from him after he left, but I wouldn't be surprised if he went to the Trappists or Carthusians.

BROTHER ROGER

Joseph   *2014*   *Roger*

One day in 1963, The Brothers of St. Joseph received an inquiry from Rhode Island. Roger was eighteen years old. Due to breathing problems, he had spent much time in the hospital as a child, but he declared he was now well enough to do a full day's work. He was of French-Canadian heritage, like myself, and I knew French-Canadian Americans in New England were of solid stock.

Brother Bill Twomey was our secretary, and I asked him to write Roger that we would accept him only upon the recommendation of his pastor. Ten days later, we received the letter.

His pastor told us Roger was a good boy, had applied at six to ten different communities, but was turned down for lack of education. He was a very religious boy, good with his hands, and merited every consideration. In his opinion we could not go wrong by accepting him.

Brother Bill and I conferred. I told him I'd have to pray on this application. I wanted to do justice by this man, but I didn't want to lower the standards of our applicants. For three days, I prayed over this application. Finally, I reasoned that the onus was on Roger. If God wanted him in our community, Roger would overcome all barriers. If not, he could leave and be none the worse—he could then go on with his life with the certitude that the life of a monk was not meant for him.

Shortly afterward when Roger arrived, his lack of education was obvious, but he seemed to make up for his limited schooling by a tremendous amount of good will and piety. He did not have a driver's license, but within a few days, he approached me to ask if I would let him take a driver's test. He passed his test with flying colors. My trust in him grew by leaps and bounds, and I never regretted giving him the green light.

Roger followed the proceedings of Vatican Council II more than any of the Brothers, so we all questioned him to learn what was happening. He was more than happy to keep us informed. Altogether, he was a member of The Brothers of St. Joseph for ten years.

Roger's first crisis showed itself about 1968 or 1969, after Vatican Council, when I had invited Sister Nativity of the Mercy Sisters for dinner and a chat. She presented herself at our front door in long tight pants, and a bright red sweater, no veil, and her two headlights on the high beam. It completely scandalized Roger, because he had lived a sheltered life, and had absolutely never seen anything as audacious as this nun. From then on, his moods wavered and he often wondered aloud, "What has the Catholic Church come to?" His mien changed completely and he began looking over the fence at girls. I think he was just a young sleeping monk, awakened from his babyhood, opening his eyes and seeing the real world for the first time. He loved what he saw, and afterward was never the same.

A Catholic carpenter from one of the local parishes offered to build a portable wood altar for Resurrection Chapel. Of course, I could not let that donation pass by: In the process of going and coming, all the brothers met the carpenter's two daughters. In a case similar to the proverbial farmer's daughter, Cerise and Roger could not take their eyes off each other and found any excuse to be alone.

I told Roger, "You are twenty-eight years old—old enough to know what you are doing. If you do not fulfill your spiritual commitments, you will surely lose your vocation." He never answered, for he could already taste the forbidden fruit. Every evening, after a hard day's work in the cemetery, he would hurry up to his room to shower and dress up. Without waiting for dinner, Roger would ask to borrow the community car for the evening, and take off in a flash.

Cerise was a beautiful girl, very mature for her age, a bank clerk—and Roger seemed proud to land such a prize. They did make a nice couple. Frankly, I had my eyes on her also! She was Roger's age—twenty years my junior. Yet I knew Roger's feeling well. In his place I might have done the same, facing that unseen force which defies control.

All the brothers in the building had in fact ceased religious community life: it was as if we were bachelors cohabiting. It is true, if you neglect your spiritual life, it deteriorates.

One evening, Roger came in from his date quite early, shortly after nine. My bedroom was downstairs, and everyone else was upstairs. I had just got into bed, and was lying awake. I must explain that our monastery was constructed all of metal—joists, partitions, everything— so every sound echoed. I heard Roger going straight upstairs to Brother Harvey's room, then both of them went into our library. Twenty minutes later, I heard Roger in his room throwing things around. I remained still. Then things quieted down.

The following morning, Roger did not come down to breakfast, so I went upstairs to check on him. He was still in bed and asked to be excused for the entire day. He had never acted that way before, but it was obvious he had some kind of trouble.

"Okay, Rodge, take the entire day," I said. I did not want to pry, figuring everything would come out in the wash.

When I came back to the office, Harvey was waiting for me. He admitted Roger had confided something to him last night. At first, Harvey didn't want to say more, but since it was obvious Roger was in trouble, I encouraged Harvey to talk.

"Typical love trouble," Harvey said.

It turns out Cerise had asked Roger if he knew the meaning of S&M. "What's that?" Rodger replied. Cerise told him to look it up in the dictionary that night, and suggested they try it out the following evening. When she would not explain, Roger stormed out.

Harvey was enrolled in college at that time, so Roger had asked Harvey's help to find the term in the dictionary.

Enlightened, I went upstairs to see how Roger was doing. "I broke up with Cerise last night," he told me.

"That's your private business, Rodge. Whatever you decide, please know you have my support, and God bless you."

I waited as long as I could—two weeks. Then, with trepidation, I called Cerise and asked for a date. I was not concerned about S&M: surely she would not bring that up, well, not on a first date. She jumped at my offer, and it made me feel good.

To avoid Cerise's dad—who was my age and my friend!—I arranged to meet her away from her house. The swankiest and most novel dining place in Oklahoma City was the 360-degree, rotating restaurant on the twentieth floor in the United Founders Tower. When we arrived, she waited for me to open her door. She got out, and hung on my arm as if for dear life. Somewhat sheltered from the dating scene due to my monk life, I was embarrassed by this display. Panicky, I resolved to get us upstairs as quickly and discreetly as possible.

Once seated, we had a wonderful conversation and I was proud to show her off in such a swanky restaurant. The view of the entire city was so beautiful from up there—it was like a fairy tale.

As we came back down by elevator, and Cerise again hung like a dead weight on my arm, I came back down to earth. In my mind I told her, *My dear Cerise, this is your first and last time.* And I say AMEN to this story.

Cerise eventually moved to Colorado, got married, and bought a ranch, which had been her wish since she was a little girl. She had one child who died at birth, and never any more. She now lives in South Dakota.

BROTHER JAMES

James was a product of the parochial school system of Wisconsin. Being attracted to the religious life, he counseled with his pastor, who suggested he write to the bishop of the Diocese for information about communities to consider. Bishop Reed wrote James a most encouraging letter, suggesting that James investigate The Brothers of St. Joseph. In line with our modus operandi, "Come and see," James visited Oklahoma.

On the day of his arrival, we had just lost our cook. James immediately replaced him, serving with distinction in the kitchen for four years.

A year before, I had sold a companion mausoleum crypt to a couple living on a ranch about an hour's drive from Oklahoma City. After seeing our life of poverty, the wife, Augusta, often brought us a bag of groceries. We became good friends with her and her husband, Slim. Slim had cancer and, shortly after, was hospitalized in St. Anthony Hospital in Oklahoma City.

One evening at 10 p.m., Augusta called from St. Anthony Hospital. "Slim is having a very hard time breathing, and I am going to stay here all night alone. Do you think Brother James could spend some time with us?"

James was there within twenty minutes. Early the following morning, a sad and drawn James returned. "Slim expired in my arms," he sobbed.

The funeral was in the parish church, with the brothers' choir singing at the mass. The committal took place in Resurrection Chapel, with Slim entombed in the garden mausoleum.

Some time later, to show her gratitude, Augusta occasionally invited the brothers to her ranch to relax. One Labor Day weekend, at Augusta's invitation, seven of our brothers piled in the car to visit the ranch. The driver, Brother George, a former baseball professional from

Kansas City, was older and supposedly more mature than the other brothers. I gave him some cash with the stipulation that they buy "something nice" for Augusta, their host. At that time I was ignorant of the fact that George had an alcohol problem. George stopped the loaded car at the first liquor store he saw and purchased a bottle of whiskey. The whiskey was shared with everyone in the car until the bottle was empty and everyone feeling good. Augusta didn't mind; she had plenty of beer, and made hamburgers in the fireplace.

Augusta had several riding horses, and encouraged the brothers to ride. Three of the brothers were from the Bronx, about nineteen or twenty years old, and had never been on horseback. One of the three, Tony, fell off his horse, breaking an arm. Augusta rushed him to the hospital and paid for all his expenses. When I saw Tony come home with his arm in a cast, I was given only the simplest explanation. Only fifteen years later, after I had left the community, did I learn the true facts of this episode. The water was already under the bridge. Oh, well!

Resurrection Cemetery was adjacent to St. Francis de Sales Minor Seminary which had over seventy-five students, and six or seven priest professors. Four sisters of the Precious Blood Order from Wichita labored in their kitchen doing all the cooking, and lifting the large pots and pans for washing. Seeing that we had many brothers working in the cemetery, the rector of the seminary asked me if I could furnish him with two brothers to help with the pots and pans in the kitchen. Brother James and another brother volunteered, remaining mainstays there for a year.

After four years with The Brothers of St. Joseph, James returned to the cooler climate of Wisconsin, where he met Margaret, his future wife. The couple enjoyed hiking through the trails and woods of Wisconsin. After their marriage, James and Margaret visited Oklahoma City several times.

After working for forty years for a state institution, on his retirement day James suffered a stroke. His lovely wife has taken care of him ever since.

We have been keeping in touch and exchanging emails regularly. For many years, Margaret has sent large Christmas packages of her own baked goods to several former Brothers of St. Joseph. James walks with difficulty, and needs much help from Margaret. Despite this, one day we learned that the couple planned to make a final visit to Oklahoma City. Several other former brothers who lived in nearby cities were notified and joined us. We all had an enjoyable reunion talking over old times.

Bless them!

Diocese of Oklahoma City and Tulsa

CHANCERY OFFICE
1921 NORTH HUDSON
OKLAHOMA CITY OKLA 73103

March 26, 1964

Mr. James J. Eggener
921 Main Street
Marinette, Wisconsin 54143

Dear James:

I was pleased to receive your letter, as I can appreciate the concern of yourself and Msgr. Bassett about your religious vocation.

The Brothers of St. Joseph are a new religious group which I feel has much promise. Brother Joseph Levesque has been in Oklahoma City over four years now, and has built a very good reputation for himself and his community. Since the community is a new one with a new ideal, it is a diocesan community with the approval of the Bishop.

In answer to your questions -- this community has my blessing and encouragement; I consider the Brothers of St. Joseph as having much promise in the future; I am sure that whoever would succeed me as Bishop of Oklahoma City and Tulsa would approve the community if it continues in the good work it is now performing. Since Brother Joseph is a solid man, there is good assurance that the community will continue and progress.

My advice to you is that you enter this community. One reason is that you have been attracted to it and its work; secondly, it will present a special challenge to you, since you are young and will be one of the pioneers of the group; again, I feel that the group gives good promise of growth and perseverance.

I will offer Mass for your intention that God may direct you according to His wisdom.

Faithfully yours in Christ,

+ Victor J. Reed

Bishop of Oklahoma City and Tulsa

Joseph, John, James, James' wife Margaret, and Tom

309

TO BURY THE DEAD

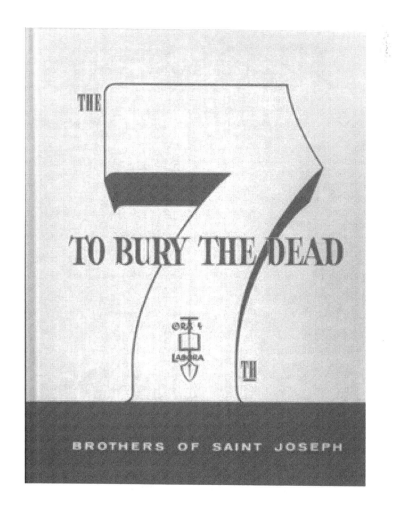

I n 1963, the Brothers of Saint Joseph published *The 7th Corporal Work of Mercy: To Bury the Dead,* whose title refers to the seventh Corporal Work of Mercy. The eighty-six-page pictorial shows the brothers at prayer, at recreation, and at work. Special emphasis is placed on Resurrection Chapel and its unique system of subfloor crypts covering the entire floor of the chapel.

Many of that book's photos illustrate stories in this book.

• • •

To Bury the Dead shows only what everything should have been. In reality, in the brotherhood were both saints and sinners. Brother Chester was only eighteen, and had already had spent two years with the Passionists. He was our first cook, and a very good one. He fabricated all our monks' habits, did the washing and ironing, and house cleaning.

At this point Brother John already had one semester at St. Gregory's college, and was one of the first four real working brothers. Mercurious brother Donald Chabot was also one of the first four working brothers, the life of the party, and a real pain in the butt. Brother Norman O'Bear (an englishized French name), was the leader of the first four best working brothers, and a real saint. The fourth man was yours truly, who was always better at giving orders, but never took second place to anyone when it came to work.

That first year, the four of us moved two cemeteries out of state, and forever basked in our glory. Those were the days of ambition and future hope. Lots of fervor, sometimes more emotional than real. Though the second wave of candidates were looked upon as "Johnnies-come-lately" and could not be looked upon as founders, they were equally dedicated. Not as adept in outdoor work as the first four, they provided the knowledge and wherewithal to make a viable community.

There was James Eggener from Wisconsin, who was the most cautious candidate we ever had. He even wrote his own bishop to see if we had any standing in the Catholic Church. A man of many abilities, he could fit in any hospital, but became our cook when the aforementioned brother Chester eloped to marry a girl he had known only two weeks.

Bill Twomey, from the Bronx, had been with some Irish teaching brothers two years where he learned the structural ropes. When he went back home, he frequented local pubs and pool halls in his neighborhood, asking old friends, "What are you going to do with your life? As for me, I'm going to enter The Brothers of St. Joseph in Oklahoma!"

Bill managed to recruit two candidates to join us even before he came to Oklahoma himself. There was a method to his good will. By sending them ahead of himself, they could act as scouts for a few weeks, and knowing that all religious communities are democratic, he was already assured two extra votes beside his vote. He was just as devious and ambitious as I was. When he arrived, I asked his background, made him my right hand man, and never regretted it.

He worked in the office full-time, answered the phone, and in my absence, he could settle any matter. It took me two months to realize that his relations to the other two New Yorkers were not so benign, but I did not say a word. His abilities overrode any negative thoughts I might have about him. I soon became dependent on him to make the community run smoothly.

It was hoped in 1963 that *To Bury the Dead* would bring in lots of vocations, but since I believe in telling things as they are, practically all the pictures in the book show the Brothers at work. Vocation literature tends to show very inviting, happy subjects, conveying the idea that everyone in the community is always happy. It is sort of misleading. Not everyone is happy all the time. Even the Pope has his moments of sadness, and days when he's down in the dumps!

In short, I've never heard of anyone joining our community by reading our book. This book and Vatican Council II contributed greatly to the demise of The Brothers of St. Joseph, plus the fact the superior was going to hell in a handbasket, and was waiting for the proper time to say au revoir.

CHAPTER 4

I AM JOSEPH, YOUR BROTHER

(John XXIII)

Then Joseph said to his brothers,
"Come close to me."
When they had done so, he said,
"I am your brother Joseph,
the one you sold into Egypt!"

Torah, Genesis 45:4

"Do not detest the Edomites or the Egyptians,
because the Edomites are your relatives
and you lived as foreigners among the Egyptians."

Bible, Deuteronomy 23:7

And when they entered upon Yusuf
he took his brother to himself;
he said, "Indeed, I'm your brother,
so do not despair over what they used to do
[to me]."

Qur'an, SURAH 12:69

ARTIFICIAL WORLD

I have no prejudice when it comes to color or faith. I love to mix with people of all colors: black of all shades, brown, white, or yellow. Also people of all faiths or no faith, the so-called atheists.

I hope to see the day when FAITH will not be a designation anymore, that we will all be believers in a Supreme Being, call HIM or HER whatever you may. And to the unbeliever, I will simply say: I AM JOSEPH, YOUR BROTHER.

We are all citizens of one world.
Why make artificial divisions in the mind.
On land: why have lines on the world map
which mean that on one side of the line is country A,
on the other side of the line is country B.
Those are all artificial lines.
If we are all citizens of one world,
WHY do we draw such lines?
It reminds me of kindergarten children
Learning to draw lines with a color crayon.
Why do we love to talk about UNITY?
when all we have in mind is that
we agree that our coffee is weak.
Let's have unity on the WORLD!
Let's have unity on the Supreme Being.
IT MADE THE WORLD, and has no sex.
What for?
Nobody knows, only The Shadow knows.

CHAPTER 5

CEMETERY

THE FINAL RIDE

Final Ride Hearse Services offers a unique and memorable experience for your cherished family members and friends; it is available to all without discrimination. The final rides that I have witnessed lead the funeral procession with dignity, honor and respect. It seems that a motorcycle hearse makes a statement, it has flair, and it personalizes the service.

Although this service is not yet available in every American city, a number of funeral directors across the country maintain a list of motorcyclists available for such an occasion.

TED & FRED

As a number of Brothers of St. Joseph left the community after Vatican Council II, we were shorthanded and turned to lay help. The first applicant we accepted was eighteen-year-old Ted, of Oklahoma Indian and Filipino heritage. A week after he started, he asked if we needed another hand; seems his kid brother was also looking for a job.

The next day Ted's seventeen-year-old brother came in, birth certificate and Social Security card in hand, to fill out an application. Both brothers were tall and of decent build, willing workers with the eagerness of youth. Their dad, who worked only two miles from the cemetery, drove them punctually to work every morning, and picked them up in the evening.

Young Fred was extremely talented. Though he had no driver's license at the time, he could drive anything, as well as repair it. He could also weld wrought iron to perfection. I saw their father every day as he delivered the two teenagers, and we soon became good friends.

Soon, the father was inviting me to lunch on Sundays. The boys' mother was Filipino, and as I had previously spent a year in Manila with the Navy, that further cemented our friendship.

One late Sunday afternoon, Ted called me and said, "You know my father, he is no more." I asked him to explain.

"It's getting warm, and this afternoon Dad decided to take the younger kids out for a swim in the river. One of the kids was drowning. When Dad jumped in the river to save him, Dad drowned. Then Hilda jumped in and saved her brother." Immediately, I thought of the parable of the Good Shepherd, willing to lose his life in order to save one sheep.

Two years later, younger brother Fred joined the Oklahoma National Guard and became a helicopter pilot. Upon his discharge, the enterprising fellow purchased his own helicopter to start a medical air evacuation service in eastern Oklahoma. One day, the helicopter wasn't functioning properly, so Fred worked on it himself and went airborne to try it out. His funeral a few days later had an overflowing church, and the following morning his cremains were buried in Resurrection Cemetery in the same grave as his father.

503

THE CROSS

In the fall of 1960, after the plans for the cemetery had been approved by Bishop Reed, heavy equipment moved in to cut roads and contour the land through the sections. The topsoil of about four or five inches was bermed at one end of the cemetery for redistribution over the sections later.

Although Oklahoma is typically windy in winter, I was told that that particular winter was the windiest in several decades. As the top soil was being scraped and hauled to the end of the property, at least half of it blew away. The hard-pan shale underneath was heavier, and most of it stayed in place. When the redistribution was finished, there were only two to three inches of soil over the hard pan.

© *To Bury the Dead*

Two years later, September 1962, we decided to erect a large redwood cross close to the entrance as a Christian symbol. Everything we did at Resurrection Cemetery was to be substantial and permanent. We certainly did not want our six-foot-wide cross, fifteen feet tall, to get blown down. To make sure it would not budge, we dug a large hole with the backhoe, and called for the concrete truck. As the concrete was setting, each one of the four brothers took his turn to scratch a memento. A few days later, we planted evergreen spreaders to cover the concrete, and provide a fine base for the cross. Time passed, and I forgot about the inscription.

• • •

Ten, twenty, thirty, forty years passed as the elements took their toll on the cross. Finally at the half-century mark, despite our previous efforts, the cross, weakened at the base, blew down to the ground. A few months later, the current cemetery crew arrived one morning to remove the spreaders and prepared to remove the concrete base. They read the old inscription on top of the concrete:

Brothers of St. Joseph
Ora et Labora
Erected Sept. 14, 1962
Feast of the Exultation of the Holy Cross

I recalled that we had scratched something on the concrete, but the exact words escaped me. Now, I realize these words were scratched on my birthday. The concrete base was removed by the cemetery crew, and the excavated hole was filled with normal soil for the time being.

Christina, the manager of the cemetery, ordered a new corpus to be placed on the cross, and three months later, the original cross was re-erected with the corpus.

ROSTAS

Julien Rostas in uniform

Former French Foreign Legionnaire, 800- and 1500-meter track champion, draftsman, machinist, and master of four languages—you name it and Julien had mastered it. Born in Budapest, Hungary, of an Austrian mother and Hungarian father, he spoke English, French, Hungarian, and German. Before World War II, Julien immigrated to France, where he met and married his wife Marcelle.

After World War II, the couple applied for immigration to the United States. Being a much-decorated war veteran on the allied side, Julien was approved quickly, and came to Oklahoma City as a machinist to work for Aero Commander, an airplane manufacturer located in nearby Bethany.

Their residence was close to ours, and we came to know them quite well. They acquired their burial plots in Resurrection Cemetery well before their need, another event that cemented our friendship. When the brothers asked about his war stories, Julien always obliged.

Having traveled all over Europe, he saw the dark clouds of an impending world war and sought to enlist in the French army. As he was not a citizen of France, he was rejected. However, noncitizens could join the French Foreign Legion. This French military unit was open to citizens of all countries, no matter their background, and was a refuge for many murderers around the world. Serving with Julien were White Russians, Germans, Hungarians, Africans, and Englishmen, but he saw no Americans during his tour of duty.

Basic training in the legion was very hard, including a 30-kilometer (about 20-mile) hike in the desert, calisthenics, and fire arms practice. His daily water ration was only one quart, and that was tough in the desert. Although private's pay was only twenty-five cents per day, Julien did so well in his spare-time work as the officers' barber, he later turned down an officer's commission. His legion unit saw action all over Europe—Germany, Norway, Africa, and Sicily.

Julien's legion career came to a close after he was decorated with France's equivalent to the Purple Heart, for grenade shrapnel wounds, and France's equivalent to the U.S. Army's Combat Infantryman Badge.

While still in Hungary, Julien worked as a draftsman in a steel tubing factory. After moving to France, he was a machinist in the Citroen and Pugeot automobile factories, then for seventeen years was foreman of twenty-eight workers with the Renault car company.

Julien and his wife received their United States citizenship papers in 1957, and were very proud to be Americans. Several years later, Julien was diagnosed with heart problems. The famous heart surgeon, Dr. Michael De Bakey, inserted a silicon valve in his heart. So far as Julien knew, he was the first person in Oklahoma City to undergo this delicate operation.

At barely sixty-five, Marcelle was diagnosed with cancer and passed away a year later. Julien, inconsolable, visited the grave daily, brought flowers, and made sure the sod on the grave was growing. Living alone, he became neurotic.

One day, he approached me and said, "Everywhere in the cemetery where you have pine trees, they are always in clusters of three. But next to Marcelle's grave, you have only two pines. Why? Why?"

"Simple, Julien. There were three of them originally, but one of them died."

"Why didn't you replace it immediately?" And so on.

It can be very hot in Oklahoma in the summer. On those days, Julien parked his car as close as possible to his wife's grave. He would lift the hood of his car "to cool the engine" and leave it up the entire time of his visit, oftentimes three or four hours. He kept a folding chair in his trunk which he set up by the grave site. The trunk lid also stayed up. He brought his own water hose to water the grass on the grave and surrounding area, including the two pine trees.

I explained this was an endowment care cemetery and the cemetery personnel maintained the entire cemetery. It didn't matter. That's the way they did it in Hungary when he was young, and that's the way he would do it now. After his watering chore, he would sit on his folding chair and read a book. Sometimes, he would pull out a blanket and take a sun bath. Several times, he intercepted a working brother to ask him to give him a rubdown with sunscreen. The brother would find an excuse and be on his way.

One very hot morning, Julien was taking his daily sun bath on his blanket, and stripped down to his undershorts to get the full benefit of the sun. These were the very short shorts, with lots of bumps. As diplomatically as I could, I pointed out several times that a cemetery was a holy place, and proper decorum should be maintained. It fell on deaf ears. On this particular day, we had a funeral scheduled for the area, and they were due in within ten minutes. The entire funeral retinue was to drive by this site, but when I apprised Julien of the impending funeral he found excuses to delay.

I looked at my watch and told him, "They will be here in exactly five minutes, and you must cover up and be respectable!"

"Let me stay here four more minutes, then I'll skiddoo."

As I was leading the funeral cortège, I breathed a sigh of relief to see, as we neared Marcelle's grave, merely a cloud of black smoke.

Julien was a wonderful man, somewhat singular, and a thorn in the side of everyone working at Resurrection Cemetery. He died in 1976, and is buried next to his wife, Marcelle, close to the two pine trees. Now, God is watering his grave every time it rains.

CHAPTER 6

OKLAHOMA AND OKLAHOMA FRIENDS

THOSE WERE THE DAYS

Those were the days. The brothers were living in Bethany next to an orphanage, ten years before Archie Bunker and his dingbat Ruth Stapleton appeared on television.

Founded in 1914, through the years St. Joseph's Orphanage nursed many good kids to adulthood. I qualify as a fellow alumnus because I was their lifeguard for several months in 1960, plus, as Superior of The Brothers of St. Joseph, for three years my community furnished the cooks for the orphanage.

A number of great achievers came out of that orphanage, which I witnessed for myself when I had the good fortune of meeting two fine gentlemen at a recent reunion of the now-grown students from St. Joseph's Orphanage.

Important in the eyes of God and the Church is alumnus Edwin "Duke" Nix, who spent all his apostolic years in Brazil. As a Brother of the Holy Cross, for three decades Duke founded schools on the Amazon in Brazil. Now retired in Oklahoma City, Duke has become one of my best friends.

Duke had a near death experience this past year that has strengthened my faith in both God and man. A lively fellow, Duke attended a party hosted by the United Way of Central Oklahoma. A guest, Michelle Rodriguez-Pico, noticed Duke collapsed on the floor after a lively round of dancing. Most fortunately, the young lady had sought training in CPR after her baby daughter choked on a grape. Rodriguez-Pico administered two rounds of chest compressions before Duke came around. Although his hospitalization led him to receive quadruple bypass surgery, my buddy is due to resume driving again in a week, and his rescuer will receive the Positive Energy Together Award from OG&E Energy Corporation.

Another fine product of St. Joseph's Orphanage is great American artist Dale Adkins, best known for his illustration of the Louis L'Amour western novels. Dale is more published than Norman Rockwell. At a recent alumni reunion, Dale Atkins generously presented attendees autographed prints of many of his paintings. Two of these (color) prints adorn the walls in my house.

© Dale Adkins

602

BAPTIST VILLAGE – STEVE AND ANGEL

Jeanine and Steve, my next door neighbors

Steve and Angel

Steve is very handy with his hands. The little white squirrel on his right (above) is made of wood and is called OVEN HELPER. It is used to pull hot oven racks towards you. It rests on two small wood rocking chairs also made by Steve.

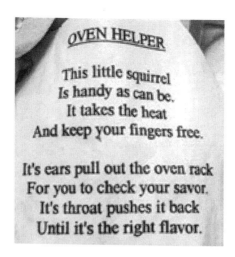

OVEN HELPER

This little squirrel
Is handy as can be.
It takes the heat
And keep your fingers free.

It's ears pull out the oven rack
For you to check your savor.
It's throat pushes it back
Until it's the right flavor.

One summer morning at six, I awoke to find the entire village out of electricity, the first time that had happened since I moved here two years ago. With a forecast high of 98, I wondered how I long I must survive with no air conditioning. And what am I going to do about breakfast? What I love on a summer morning is iced coffee. At the Walmart just around the corner, I often pick up a four-pack of iced coffee or cappuccino. In semi-darkness I went to the refrigerator and pulled out a bottle of iced coffee.

When I opened the front door to a beautiful seventy-five-degree morning, the rocking chair on my front patio looked very appealing.

It's dead quiet outdoors and indoors, with only an occasional car driving by.

I normally keep on hand a bottle of coffee liqueur, and spike my iced coffee with half an inch of it—it gives me an ounce of pep to start my day—but I had run out of all liqueurs. I looked all around, and all I had was a miniature bottle of viper brandy that my neighbor Steve had helped me to recap due to evaporation. But I had two bottles of standard size viper brandies—worth their weight in gold, so I would never touch them. This little miniature viper brandy is expendable, so I can drink the brandy and leave the baby snake in the bottle, and replace the brandy later.

I shook the bottle so it would be evenly mixed, and poured a shot of miniature viper brandy into my bottle of iced coffee, taking it with me out to the front patio where I sat in my rocking chair to enjoy the morning fresh air. One sip of my iced coffee told me I had a whopper. I drank almost the entire bottle, and was feeling good.

From down the street to my left, neighbor Steve was coming back from walking his dog, Angel, as he does every morning. Angel is a one-man dog and will not let me touch her, yet she is adorable. Sometimes I think she is human. Of course, as they got closer to my patio, Steve released Angel from the leash, and she came running to me, and stopped about ten feet away to bark at me. She was telling me something. She sniffed the air, acting a little strange. By the time Steve reached me and sat down on the brick wall, Angel was somewhat closer than usual, and sniffing more than usual.

Steve may have assumed I was drinking my usual summer iced coffee, but I told him that today it was spiked with mini viper brandy from the same little bottle he helped me with two months ago. He smiled to remember our little project.

I enjoy my morning encounters with Steve.

Steve is an angel as well as his dog. When I get sick, he watches over me. I have no relatives in Oklahoma City, so Steve runs errands for me. He will go to the pharmacy, and even bring my meals when I am in bed. He has the keys to my house and I trust him implicitly. I would love to repay him in kind, but he is younger than I am.

"I have a feeling of exhilaration," I told Steve. I raised my glass in a toast to the morning. "I'm sorry it's almost all gone."

Steve thought I was only joking, because I kid him a lot. "Angel loves coffee also," he said. "Once in a while, I give her a little sip, and she really laps it up."

"Let me give her the rest of my bottle, and give her a little pleasure also!"

"No way, Joe! I simply don't want to see what might happen!"

"I have only one gulp left. I'll share it with Angel by pouring a few drops on the sidewalk."

Steve obviously thought, "Joe's full of baloney, pulling my leg as usual."

He was indoors with Angel for only a moment when his door flew open, and Angel rushed outdoors onto the grass to let something out of her mouth. Steve called out to me, "Darn it, Joe, you weren't foolin'! Angel got sick on that spiked brandy."

Seeing that, I resolved never to spike my iced coffee again.

My little Angel

BAPTIST VILLAGE

Joseph   *Chaplain Chris*

One day, Chaplain Chris came to visit me in my home at Baptist Village. Though we had already met, we had not yet had a good conversation, so this day made up for lost time. I opened my heart to him, and began telling him my entire life's story: my education, joining the U.S. Navy (he told me his father had done the same thing), the Snowshoers, the Cistercians, The Brothers of St. Joseph, Resurrection Cemetery, leaving the Catholic Church for forty years, and so on. As a token of our friendship, he gave me the Bible as seen in the above photo.

I am absolutely convinced he is a man of God.

As Chaplain Chris left the house, we were both convinced God was calling me to the ministry. As soon as I closed the door, my eyes, mind, and heart became distracted by a beer bottle displayed on my shelf in the entryway. It had a very intriguing label and a very interesting story behind the label—thunderclap!

Now I know what God wants me to do—to simply continue what I have been doing the past forty years—writing about bottle labels. For me it is mentally rewarding.

When Chaplain Chris returned the following week, I told him I was returning to the faith of my fathers, and continuing my monthly magazine writings: "There is a story behind every label." He has been most understanding—more so than the dignitaries of my institutional church.

I love it here at Baptist Village. Yesterday morning, I left my house at 8 a.m., heading for my car parked across the street. To cross the street, I had to walk across the sidewalk, traverse twelve feet of verdure (grass) and jump a good-sized curb. My balance went atwitter, and I fell down. I am dead weight when I fall down, and I can't get up by myself. That's why I carry a caller wrung around my neck, but I preferred not to use it that morning because they might send an ambulance or a firetruck. I felt someone would see me, and lend a hand.

A young man whom I had never seen before, was on his way to work. From a distance, he saw me fall and drove his car near me, lowered his window, and asked, "Need a hand, friend?"

"All I need is a hand to get up and I can walk on my own two feet!"

The young man got out of this car, and before he could even touch my hand, three neighbors approached, also ready to give me a hand. Seeing that, I cried. To me, all these hands were the hands of God reaching for mine. Oh! I love it here at Baptist Village.

Later that morning, Chaplain Chris told me, "Yes, they were the hands of God and Oklahoma. You will find all the hands of Oklahoma will always reach out for you." How true. Oh! I love it here at Baptist Village and Oklahoma!

Maria De Lorea with a Baptist Village resident

Honorable mention must be made of Maria De Lorea, activities director at Assistance in Living at Baptist Village. She helps residents enjoy special musical activities, crossword puzzles, and conversational times in the day room. She assists residents to play cards, go on trips around Oklahoma, and generally keeps the Assistance in Living department well-oiled.

Come on guys, don't get your dander up! Maria is already spoken for.

LENA

ena was Rita's junior sister—ten years difference. I met her in the 1980s when she was living in northeast Oklahoma City on land owned by Rita. (You'll run into Rita when you read about Byron's.) Rita owned half of a frontage block, where she had a beautiful estate house made of clinkered bricks with a three-car garage and all the amenities. Lena lived on the opposite corner down the street in a more modest home. Another sister lived on the opposite corner on property also owned by Rita. Get the picture? Lena used to call Rita the "rich bitch," but they were civil to each other, and got along for appearance's sake.

Lena owned an ugly cross-eyed bulldog which she loved as if it was her own baby. I visited her there only twice, being prudent not to get crossed between the two loving sisters and the cross-eyed bulldog.

When Rita passed away in 1955, her estate was sold, outstanding bills were paid, and the balance willed to the Carmelite nuns. It supported them for several years.

Lena's property was sold from out from under her. So she purchased another house in Hefner Village in northwest Oklahoma City. Once installed there, she decided to replace Rita in my life, and I wasn't too keen on that—I'd had enough of that de Lasalle Cajun family. Try as I may, Lena kept dropping in at my house, two miles from hers, at any time of day or night. She never rang the bell, she'd just walk in and start her monolog. One night, in my bedroom I awoke hearing what I thought was conversation in the living room. There was Lena, installed in my favorite easy chair, talking a mile a minute. To whom? Damned if I knew.

Each day was a repeat of the previous, more of the same. As the saying goes, the more things change, the more they stay the same. What a life I had! To escape the everyday humdrum, I began traveling to France two weeks out of every month, doing some bootlegging. I absolutely never told Lena nor anyone else.

One day Lena complained to me about cracks in her concrete driveway and asked if I could fix it. I offered to purchase filler caulk at Home Depot to take care of it.

The following morning, I was sitting on the concrete, filling cracks under Lena's supervision. Up the street came a neighbor, Maxine, on her daily walk. Lena leaned over to hiss at me, "Don't you dare talk to that bitch." With a straight face, I answered, "Don't worry."

As soon as Maxine reached the driveway, she began to talk to me—we knew each other well, and I was fond of her. Lena was hiding behind her own car in the garage, stretching her neck and ears, so as not to miss anything, good or bad—in her opinion usually bad. At last, she could not bear it any longer. She came out on the driveway and with her over-emoted smile, she greeted Maxine with an emotional, "Hi, my lovely Maxine! It's so-o-o nice to see you! How I lo-o-ove to see you early in the mornings. You make my day!"

I strained myself trying to keep a straight face.

Lena always loved to chat with me—or at me, since it was always one way—and she prided herself in telling me she was worth more than Rita when she died, but I think that was just hot air.

Lena and Rita had always competed in everything, and since Rita bought a brand new Cadillac every year, Lena would buy a brand new Lincoln Town Car each year. She loved to remind me the Town Car was bigger than the Cadillac, and for once she was right.

One day, Lena had an accident with her brand new Town Car. Just a fender bender, but holy smoke, it would cost $9,000 to fix, and she did not have that kind of money. Her statement to the police contradicted the statement by the other driver.

When the other driver approached her with his insurance information, she had a fit of apoplexy and I had to call an ambulance. She was driven to the hospital—where she died two days later. I was left to make all arrangements and settle the estate.

Wait a minute! My tale of woe is not finished.

Along with her attorney, I proceeded to fulfill her wishes: to pay off all her just debts, and then distribute her estate as she wished. She left me the damn Lincoln Town Car with the fender bender intact, and graced charity with the balance.

God bless her. The attorney, Le Roy, suggested I make out the checks and he would deliver them to her favorite charities himself. I wasn't born yesterday!

"Over my dead body!" I retorted. "We will deliver the checks together!" So we proceeded to make the distribution together. The last check, for close to a half million dollars, was going to St. Ann's Nursing Home.

The attorney said he would prefer that we leave the check at the Archdiocesan business office. "I know Dave Johnson, the business manager," he said. "I used to work with his dad, also an attorney, at the Internal Revenue Service."

So he introduced me to Dave Johnson, who was very pleasant. We talked a little about Resurrection Cemetery, I presented Dave the big check, and our visit ended. Attorney Le Roy and I congratulated each other for a job well done. THE END? Not yet.

Two days later, Dave Johnson called me. "Mr. Levesque, I think you made that check on the wrong account!"

"How could I have made it on the wrong account, when there was only one account"?

"There is a problem with the check." I didn't ask what it was. That was HIS problem.

Two days later, Dave called again. "Mr. Levesque, I apologize for calling you the other day. We found the problem."

"What was it?"

"Oh, we're still working on it!"

There was something fishy in Denmark. So I called attorney Le Roy and explained the situation.

"Oh, don't worry about it, Joe. It will all come out in the wash."

"Well, Le Roy, not my wash. I'll work my way to the bottom of this."

"Frankly, Joe, the check was paid by the bank and it was un-endorsed."

"That's impossible, Le Roy, you know that!"

"I am told it was done."

"What can I do?"

"Just keep mum."

I tried to go to the bottom of this...but it was so contorted. Half a million dollars is no small amount. The sloppiness and flagrant inefficiencies of the bank dealing with St. Ann's Nursing Home may have resulted from too many hands in the pot. Eventually, in absolute disgust, I dropped it.

VANANTWERPEN

F rans and Sonja were born and married in Holland. Early on, Frans went into the chemical business, then founded Akxo Corporation. In 1960, they decided to move to the United States. They hired a moving company to transport the forty containers holding their personal belongings, furniture, Akxo office equipment, and papers—by ship. After living in two other American cities, they settled on Oklahoma City, because this city and state have lots of chemical interests.

In Oklahoma City, Frans and Sonja became acquainted with John and Rita. John was a Dutchman, and Rita was Indonesian, but she spoke Dutch quite well (see chapter "Rita" in *Monk to Bootlegger*). I met Frans and Sonja through John and Rita.

It seems that Frans decided to retire and sold most of his stock in Akxo. Impressed by these facts, I can only conclude that Frans is a millionaire. I have never said so viva voce, and if they ever hear I said it, both Frans and Sonja would be upset and remonstrate with me.

They once purchased a miniature cobra wine in Laos for 2 USD; enjoyed possessing it for twenty years; then tried to peddle it to no avail. When they finally turned to me, wanting $100, I offered only fifty—and it was no way, Jose! So they kept their cobra brandy, and I resolved not to try to push a deal, because I own six other cobra brandies and do not have a hole in my head to own another one.

Sonja is a real lady. One day as we were having lunch at Cajun King restaurant in Oklahoma City, she overheard my conversation. I had just told the owner, "Please don't bool-sheet me anymore!"

Sonja, in her heavy Dutch accent, remonstrated with me: "Yosef, that's not a nice word to say to anyone. You hurt that poor man's feelings!"

I fumed. Who in hell does she think she is? My mother? She's younger than I am! I have reached the age of reason. She may be a millionairess, but feelings have no pricetag! In deference to Sonja, I eventually came down from my ivory tower. I may rant as I wish, but she accomplished her purpose: I haven't spoken those words since that day. Thank God, Sonja is making a gentleman out of me.

A few years ago, Frans and Sonja were visiting Scandinavia, and visited the Eidfjord Museum in Norway. They saw these four beautiful paintings of monks, thought of me, and photographed them. Wasn't it nice of them to do that? Here are the pictures they took.

MY MUSLIM FRIENDS

Muslims are in the United States to stay. It's a fact—the process of assimilation is ongoing. They are to be found in all our cities and many are engaged in the professions, such as medical, educational, and the hospitality sector. Their children go to American schools, learning English the American way. In the larger cities, many Muslim communities have their own schools, not unlike Catholics who have their own parochial school system. Muslim schools must follow guidelines from their community board of education, just as public schools and parochial schools do.

My first real Muslim friend in Oklahoma City was Rachid. I met him years ago at his restaurant that goes by the name of Couscous Cafe. Sometime later, I met his wife. I had heard wild descriptions about Muslim women, so before meeting her, I asked Rachid about the protocol to follow in greeting her. He laughed.

"Just be normal! She won't hurt you. Act like you are meeting an American woman for the first time."

One morning, I went to Rachid's other restaurant, Istanbul, one hour before it opened, to talk to Rachid in private, without the pressures of business. He wasn't there, but instead I saw a woman with a black shawl on her head, baking Turkish bread over an open hearth flame. I approached her as much as I could from my side of the counter.

"You must be Rachid's wife."

She turned to me with a beautiful smile. "Yes, I am."

"I am Joseph the Bootlegger."

"I've heard so much about you, I feel I already know you quite well." Her English was better than her husband's.

"What's your name, ma'am?

"My name is Khadija!"

"How do you spell it?"

"K-H-A-D-I-J-A."

An animated, half-hour conversation ensued, releasing me from my inhibition about talking to Muslim women. Yes, they are like American women!

I learned Rachid was away delivering a catered lunch to the Raindrop Turkish House, so I went there to chat with him. The president of the Oklahoma City Chamber of Commerce was about to speak at the event, so Rachid found me a chair, where I enjoyed the program.

With Rachid's two Middle Eastern restaurants, he is having his having his slice of the great American Pie. May Allah be with him!

• • •

At Istanbul, I made other Muslim friends. Amr, a Slovak born on the outskirts of Sa'na, Yemen, was accepted into the United States on a Slovak student visa. Yemen—the birthplace of the Arab world—was never occupied by the French (or any other country), so Amr doesn't speak French. Amr is young, and a fast learner. He reminds me of our Brother John of the Brothers of Saint Joseph: the same physique, the same understanding smile, a saintly mien. I believe Brother John to be a Catholic saint, and Amr to be a Muslim saint.

Joseph and Amr at the mosque in Oklahoma City

Another Muslim friend is Adnane, owner of Argana restaurant, which serves Moroccan cuisine. There, Chef Mostapha (Adnane's brother-in-law) makes wonderful tajines, gyros, kababs, and the like.

Adnane   *Mostapha*

Abdul also works at Argana and for the past several years has been begging me to write a book with him. His part would be about the Muslims, and my part would about be Christians. Frankly, if I had negative thoughts about Christians, I would not convey them to Muslims.

Abdul   *Rita*

All four of these fellows have been my friends for several years. Most of them are from Morocco, all are devout Muslims. What do I—a Christian—have to lose from their acquaintance? My faith? If I lose my faith, then I may not have had it in the first place.

• • •

Dr. Hassoun, my urologist, from Kuwait, is also a Muslim, and I have learned that all five of these men attend the same mosque in Oklahoma City. My first visit to the mosque was initiated by Adnane, who asked me to accompany him there one day.

After that, I began visiting the mosque each Friday, and there I meet new people. Before my first visit, a dozen questions came to mind. Any special dress? Do I have to wash my feet with them? Will they all be watching me? Do I have to say anything? Do I have to pray with them?

These concerns amounted to nothing when I walked in. Adnane took his shoes off at the entrance, and so did I. No one even looked at me. Everyone was doing his routine paying no attention to anyone else. What an exhilarating feeling it was! For me as a Catholic, it was like walking out of the confessional after a particularly good confession.

In all the times I've been to the mosque, I've never seen a donation basket being passed around. There was a big question mark in my mind, so I asked a Muslim friend, why not? He answered that there is no need for it, and explained the Five Pillars of Islam.

SHAHADA: FAITH

SALAT: PRAYER

ZAKAT: ALMSGIVING

SAWM: FASTING

HAJJ: PILGRIMAGE TO MECCA, at least once in a lifetime

In ZAKAT (Almsgiving), the donation should benefit the community where you live. The giving should be in kind. If the person needs flour, you should give flour. There's absolutely no precept to give to the mosque. Usually, the sheik provides for the mosque, and in Oklahoma City, a rich Muslim provided for the mosque. I always have this info in my mind when I go to the mosque and keep my money in my pockets. I keep my mind on Allah, it seems to be releasing...like being born again...like being in a new world. Then you wake up, and the imam starts the prayers. The prayers are always in Arabic, the language of Muhammad. Those said, the imam delivers his sermon in the language of our country. Most of these men are American citizens who live among us; whose children go to school with our children; whose wives buy their food at the supermarket shoulder to shoulder with our wives. Someday we shall all hear Gabriel's trumpet recalling us to the bosom of the One Who Made Us. Together, we shall climb Muhammad's ladder to Heaven.

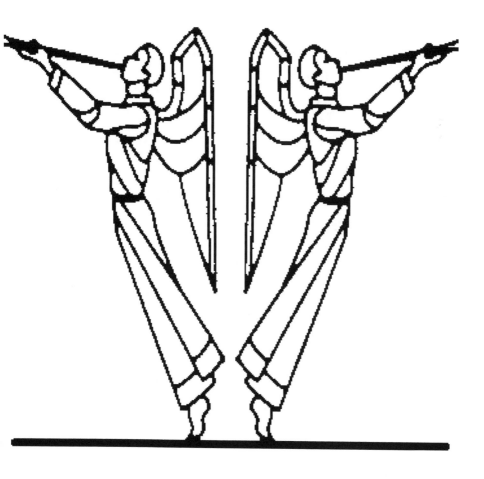

WHIRLING DERVISHES

The whirling dervishes came to my attention in World War II as I was touring the world in the U.S. Navy. It was fascinating to watch these men dancing to an oriental beat. For a sailor, this was only entertainment for a night, with tomorrow bringing new adventures. The dervishes were soon forgotten in the far recesses of a whirling mind.

Whirling dervishes at Rumi Fest 2007

In 2013, as I was exiting a Walmart, some teenagers at the parking lot entrance were handing out fliers for an event at the Raindrop Turkish House—featuring whirling dervishes! Ted French and I could not pass that up, even though Ted doesn't like dirty Arabs. We have been arguing for years: Who is dirtier, Arabs or Americans? I always tell him, if you knew their religion, you would quickly find they are cleaner than we are.

The event was very entertaining, and what an education! They are a religious order, as the Brothers of St. Joseph were.

Whirling dervishes trace their origins back to the thirteenth century Ottoman Empire. Dervishes are Sufi Muslims, a sect found mostly in Turkey, who tend to be ascetics and mystics. Most are men, but occasionally you may find a group of women. Individuals belong to orders (similar to the Catholics such as the Franciscans and Benedictines). The largest of these orders is the Mevlevi order, the ones we see performing for educational purposes and the tourist trade.

Each twist of the hands and the head has a spiritual meaning, and a dervish recites devotional Islamic prayers while whirling. As the ritual dance begins, the dervish dons a felt cap, in addition to a turban wrapped around the head, a trademark of the Mevlevi order. The dance of the dervishes is one of the most impressive features of the mystical life in Islam, and the music accompanying it is of exquisite beauty.

I shall never miss the occasion of attending one of these swirling dances, because I place myself in their shoes and pray in unison with them. There are so many nice features in Islam! Sometimes I feel ashamed of being Christian.

CIRCUS PARENTS

by
Dawn Mahiya

Remember those old-time stories you used to read where young people would run off to join the circus? That's exactly what my parents did in 1962! The summer after he got out of the army, my twenty-one-year-old father joined the circus at one of its stops in Michigan. Fortunately, my adventurous mother happened to join a few months later, at just nineteen, and so there, under the big top, my parents met!

The circus they joined—Clyde Beatty-Cole Brothers—was the largest "under the big top" circus traveling up and down the east coast of the United States. Under its current name, Cole

Brothers Circus remains the largest circus in the world still performing under a "big top" tent. Formerly the circus traveled and performed only along train routes, using rail cars for transport, but by 1957, it had transitioned to traveling in a mile-long cavalcade of trucks. This permitted visits to many more towns along the east coast than in previous years, and Cole Brothers remained a major player in the circus industry for the next several decades.

A typical playbill from 1962 showed entertainment headed by Clyde Beatty and his group of trained lions and tigers; La Norma, an aerialist known as Denmark's Goddess of Balanced Flight; the Genoas flying trapeze artists; Barton, a man who stands on his forefinger; and the Jordans and Victors novelty aerial acrobats. An added attraction was "double-flight human cannonball" Captain Astronaut!

My father trained and performed as a fire-eater and my mother trained and performed in the "Electric Act" and in the blade box. My mother told me that the magician she was assistant to in the Electric Act had such a drinking problem that she often feared for her life. In the Electric Act my mother stood on an electrified metal plate hidden on the floor. When the magician handed her an electric bulb, it would magically light up in my mother's hand. Other objects were also placed in her hand that she would "electrify." The problem was, she was specifically instructed to never touch the microphone the magician was using because that would ground the electrical charge, electrocute and probably kill her. No problem, except that during the show, the tipsy magician kept accidentally trying to hand her the forbidden microphone. She said it was quite challenging to stay in character while dodging the deadly mic. That I was born proves she somehow managed to keep her job while avoiding electrocution.

Plenty of hard labor is involved in circus life. The performers, especially new people who joined only for a season, were all required to help care for the animals—mucking out manure from animal stalls, hauling water, feed, and bedding materials to the animals—and to help get the tents put up. My mother was written up in the newspaper in one town after she discovered that one of the hippos had escaped its pen and was running around loose.

Many of the circus workers actually bunked with the animals. My father shared the giraffe's pen with another guy. My father often worked with the elephants, who helped erect the huge tents the circus performed under. Several of these elephants had young, which despite being small, were still very powerful and could accidently kill a man with one blow. Although Clyde Beatty repeatedly warned my father not to interact with these calves, my father loved to play with them. One day my father was encouraging the smallest baby elephant to swing its trunk up and down to slap my father's hand. The elephant became very excited and hit my father on the head instead of on his hand! Twenty-four hours later my father woke up with a concussion—and a very angry animal trainer. Clyde Beatty then moved my father to work with other animals who didn't have any young to play with.

Every circus performer was encouraged to cross-train with other acts to be ready—just in case—to take over if one of the other performers was injured. Both of my parents trained in the trapeze acts and the tightrope acts.

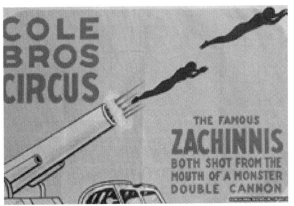

My mother also trained with Hugo Zacchini, "The Human Cannonball." Hugo wasn't performing that season, as the previous year he'd had a mid-air collision with his wife Elsbeth during a performance, and they were both injured. Hugo's wife's injury unfortunately required her to use a wheelchair for the rest of her life.

My mother was trained for the cannon stunt and then was shot out of the cannon once. She told me she was told to take one last look at the target net, climb down inside the cannon, and then keep her head down and prepare for the blast that would send her from zero to about fifty miles an hour in one-fifth of a second. A lot had to happen in that four seconds between when the cannon fired and when she was going to land. She had to recognize the way she came out of the cannon and correct her flight in order to do a somersault before she came crashing into the net. Except that's not what happened.

My mother's once-in-a-lifetime thrill as a human cannonball wannabe began after she climbed into the cannon and held her head down waiting for the blast to occur. Nothing happened for a while, and just as she lifted her head to ask about the delay, the cannon fired. Her head hit the top of the cannon and knocked her out. Hugo was horrified to see a limp body shooting toward the net, sure he was going to have a dead performer on his hands. Luckily, my mother recovered from the blow just in time for a last minute somersault to land on her back in the net. She was shaken and bruised, not having landed exactly right, but she was alive. Both The Human Cannonball and my mother agreed that maybe the cannon act wasn't good "fodder" for her to continue in cross-training.

My parents traveled and performed with Clyde Beatty-Cole Bros Circus until they arrived in its winter training grounds in DeLand, Florida. DeLand is located midway between Orlando and Daytona Beach. My parents wintered with the circus and trained for the next season, but eventually decided not to continue on with the upcoming circus tour. After marrying in Sarasota in May 1963, they moved back to Michigan by Christmas to be near family. My father found work in the steel mill and my mother hired on at Macy's as a security guard.

They both felt the skills they had learned in the circus were useful, and they taught my sister and me what they had learned. I grew up learning how to fall properly (so as not to be injured when training), how to walk a tightrope, how to perform on a trapeze, how to ride a unicycle, how to handle electricity, and how to handle various animals and reptiles. My parents revealed many of the tricks magicians use to trick the viewers' eyes and even trained us how to do some of them! Although my father considered me too young to learn to "eat fire," he delighted us by amazing our guests with his fire-breathing prowess. He explained to me the most important thing about the skill, namely: Don't breathe in when the fire is lit!

In 1998, my college class syllabus warned that an upcoming assignment would require students to write a sixteen-page children's book. Before it could be assigned, I began writing the book, beginning with the story of my circus parents. I exceeded the sixteen pages and begged the professor for permission to write twice as much, yet still had to cut down the tale to limit it to 10,000 words. I have shared this little book with quite a few of my friends. When Joseph looked at it, he said that since a picture is worth a thousand words, my 150 photos in the book are the equivalent of 150,000 words. I have since added to my story, hoping to publish it someday as the initial chapter of my autobiography.

Note: Dawn works as a home inspector for her living, is a well-known Argentine tango dancer in Oklahoma City, and sings in the Paseo Arts District in the local band Tango Posse. She is also a good helper to Joseph.

CHAPTER 7

LIQUORS

PRINCIPALITY OF ANDORRA

A ndorra is a sovereign, landlocked microstate in the Eastern Pyrenees mountains, sandwiched between France and Spain. The sixth smallest nation in Europe, Andora consists of only 181 square miles, and boasts the highest capitol city in Europe.

The official language is Catalan, although Spanish, Portuguese, and French are also spoken. If you hear English, it has to be from a tourist or business person, whom everyone will understand. It is the crossroad of Europe, specializing in illegal activity and illicit sales.

Andorra's tourism is estimated at 10.2 million visitors annually. While Andorra is not a member of the European Union, the euro is the de facto currency. Go in a store, and bargain for some goods, and they will accept all currencies. The people of Andorra have one of the highest life expectancies in the world, according to *The Lancet*—eighty-one years of age in 2013. Apparently, the cold is good for your body!

The Andorra Mountains

There are several hundred hotels in Andorra, and I've never worried about making reservations. You'll always find a room. Lodging is geared mostly to the winter ski season, but I've always visited in summer. There are no airports or rail services. I don't know how tourists make it up there in the winter! I presume they go by bus. When roads are slippery, smaller vehicles follow a truck with snowplow attached. Accommodations for weather are a fact of life, and no one there seems to mind. There is a long serpentine road from France to Andorra, but if you are queasy about heights, don't go!

Andorra's serpentine road

When I used to go up to Andorra in summer in a rental car, it took me three hours from the last French city to the first city in Andorra. That was in the 1980s. At that time, Absinthe was banned in every country in the world except Russia and Andorra. I would have been a fool to go to Russia, especially when Andorra was so close and easy. I especially loved the capitol city, Andorra la Vella. Typically, I checked into a hotel right away and lay down after my three hours of driving and concentrating. After chilling a while, I would get up and find the closest liquor store. They all carried Absinthe at a ridiculously low price. I would buy five or six bottles, then hasten back to my room. The bottles went straight into the bathtub with lots of hot water. After a half-hour soak, the labels were floating in the bathtub. I plucked the labels out and placed them on the radiator to dry. I then dried and cleaned each bottle with a bath towel, and let them stand. Next came a walk into town. That thirty minutes to an hour gave me an opportunity to scout out my environment.

When I returned to my room, it was time to affix my own labels on these unmarked bottles. I had to choose labels for a colorless liquor, such as vodka or marc. This was the easy part. After gluing my own labels, they stood for the night, drying.

In the morning, the newly labeled bottles went into a large box first, then they were covered with licit bottles, and off I went. It took about 2.5 hours coming down the serpentine roads, in second gear all the way, all the while watching for La Police Volante. They would stop me when I least expected them. After all, they were experts, and I was the neophyte.

After the viewing of my identification came the regular search. They looked at every bottle, but when they reached the new labels, I would pull my ancestry gig on them: We were all Frenchmen, and they were now my friends. It always distracted them, and my inspection was over. History repeated itself.

My next hurdle was U.S. Customs at Kennedy Airport. But that was easy. American customs would not know a licit label from an illicit label. I never worried.

When back home, I repeated the process in reverse. Bottles that cost me $2 in Andorra, could be sold for $300 to $500. Try to match the risks against the profits! Was it worth it?

I don't know.

All I can say is that I started penniless, and I ended up penniless. It is like being born again. I came into this world with nothing, and I will be leaving with nothing. Blessed be the Lord.

LA POLICE VOLENTE
(The Flying Squad)

La Police Volente de France, part of the National Police, is the bane of all drivers in France. Their jurisdiction covers all of France, and they have much more power than state police in the United States. They are entrusted with the borders of France, proper identification, contraband, illegals, etc. The same power covers ports and airports. When they patrol the autoroutes, they are called La Police Volente. When I drove on the autoroutes following the speed laws (not always), they would pass me in a flash. Where they were going, nobody knew. I never understood why speed limits do not apply to them. Beware; if they are after you, they'll get you whether you are holed up in a small country hotel, in bed or in the bathtub.

Members of the Police Nationale during the July 14, 2011 parade in Toulon, France

The Flying Squad passes in review

This photo presents the motorcycle police in dress uniform. On the autoroutes, their dress consists of a black leather jacket, black leather pants, black leather boots, and a white G-man strap at the waist and across the chest.

On the border between Andorra and France are no visible police, nor customs agents. The borderline is somewhere along the serpentine road going from France to Andorra. At least the French were rational in this situation. Coming down from the Pyrenees, stopping would be difficult and might cause an accident. La Police Volente usually patrol at the bottom of the Pyrenees: I've driven through there at least thirty times, and they were never at the same place. They usually have roadblocks, and when traffic backs up, another group of police sets up a roadblock farther down.

They come to your car for identification and search. Woe to you if your papers are not in order or if you have contraband items. You lose your car, right then and there. How you get back home is your problem. Of course, any human sharks patrolling the highways and byways fare no better!

La Police Volente has questioned and searched me every time I've been to Andorra, and I've always been careful to be polite ("No, sir!" "Yes, sir!") but it is my ancestry that is the lifesaver, mentioned at the right time.

But thinking of trying to pass La Police Volente with four or five bottles of contraband Absinthe still causes me to break out in a sweat. One day, I almost poo-pooed in my pants when the questioning came close to the negative, and my shirt was soaked. It is always quite the relief to pass La Police Volente.

GASCONY

A map of Gascony, showing a wide definition of the region. Other maps may define a smaller area as Gascony.
(Map by Larrousiney)

Gascony, in my estimation, must have the best climate in the world to grow grapes because they have the very best red wine for your health—as certified by scientists in France and England. Next to Saint Joan of Arc, the Gasconais have given the greatest saint to the Catholic Church in France, in the person of Bernadette Soubirous, the inspiration for the 1943 movie, *The Song of Bernadette*.

Gascony is also known for its Armagnac brandy. Even though Cognac was my specialty, I must confess that I much prefer the taste of Armagnac. It has a more complex taste, the taste of terroir (an earthy taste). It is distilled only once in a continuous still, while Cognac is distilled twice in a pot still. This second distillation seems to lose the esters and phenols, making it harsh to the taste. To me, Armagnac is more mellow with a greater, richer, and more savory taste.

Gascony is extremely rich in history and culture, and especially in good food. It is the land of duck, foie gras, confit, and the Three Musketeers. It was the home of perhaps France's greatest and most popular king, Henri IV, in the sixteenth century. (If you have the opportunity to read about his life, please do so.) This land of rolling and dense hills is replete with hiding places, so it is not surprising that it was a hotbed of the French Resistance during World War II. Tiny villages are infused with a sense of the past and authenticity; its people have a sense of belonging and sharing.

Typical view of the hilly countryside of Gascony, with the Pyrenees mountains in the far distance

For ages, Gascony has had a special soup called garbure. The name sounds so much like garbage that I avoided it for years, but how wrong I was! *Merriam-Webster* describes it as a thick soup of bacon and cabbage or other vegetables, usually with cheese and stale bread added. It is akin to our vegetable soups, but I would take ten garbures to one of our vegetable soup. It is delicious to look at, and more so to devour. In the south of France, if you see garbure on the menu, try it, you'll like it.

Garbure: Ham, cabbage and other vegetables, cheese, stale bread

The wines of Madiran are also well known as the most healthy of red wines due to the high levels of procyanidin they contain. Scientists have found this wine to be good for reducing blood pressure, lowering cholesterol and encouraging healthy blood clotting. The village of Moirax also has very good wines.

BYRON'S LIQUOR WAREHOUSE

Byron's casks

Two weeks after I arrived in Oklahoma City in 1960, I received a visit from Brother Gabriel. His community, the Brothers of Mercy, operated St. Vincent's Nursing Home on East 23rd Street. When he arrived to welcome me to Oklahoma, I sheepishly pulled out an old straight chair covered in storage dust.

"Brother Gabriel, I regret I cannot offer you a better seat. I've been alone here for two weeks, and you are the first Religious to visit me. I surely appreciate you dropping by."

We ended up having a one-hour conversation.

"Have you met Rita Grimm yet?" Brother Gabriel asked. I had not. "She has been our best benefactress, and don't worry, she will find you before you try to find her."

Later on Rita found me and immediately proceeded to take me under her wing. I told her about my Cistercian background, the reason I could never accept alms from her. Without batting an eye, she kept talking: She was practically supporting the Brothers of Mercy, and had even given them a pickup truck. However, I would not condone her meddling in our affairs, and told her so.

A week or two later, Rita mentioned that her late mother's name was de La Salle, making her a descendant of Le Sieur de La Salle, the purported discoverer of the Mississippi River. Although her entire family were a hundred percent Cajun, in the course of being active in business they had eventually lost their French language. When I learned her mother was buried in Oklahoma City's Memorial Park, I perceived Rita was caught between a rock and a hard place—for now that the diocese was establishing Resurrection Cemetery, it was apparently too late for her mother to be buried there.

I told her what I could do. Bear in mind that in earlier days, rather than purchase a single or double plot, a person would customarily purchase a cemetery lot that could hold the entire family. I made Rita an offer: for her twelve-grave lot in the costly Memorial Park, she would receive a twelve-grave lot in the Catholic-blessed Resurrection Cemetery—and I would accomplish the transfer of her mother's remains at no cost to her. This offer, she could not refuse. That sealed our friendship.

It was then that Rita explained to me what had transpired in the previous five years.

Rita's mother owned a Cajun-American Restaurant on the corner of Northeast 23rd Street and Broadway. For years—long before World War II—Rita operated a tire shop across the street on the southeast corner of 23rd and Broadway. In the early 1940s, she happened to acquire a carload of tires. You can see that when the war came along and tires were rationed, she stood to make a ton of money. At the war's end in 1945, being smugly rich and self-sufficient, Rita chose to retire. Although she kept the property, her best worker, Joe Esco, bought the business from her and within a couple of years, Joe had four or five stores around Oklahoma City.

At about that time, an old friend of Rita's, Byron Gambulos, approached her about forming a partnership with him to open a liquor establishment on Joe Esco's corner. Oklahoma was a dry state at the time, but Byron assured her liquor was coming in soon; he wanted a partner, and Rita was the one. Rita figured she was now retired, and would not go back in business, Byron or no Byron. So Byron promptly purchased the corner property from her and started constructing a store. He was very protective of Rita, and word never got out that the land was purchased from her. (And as for the displaced Joe Esco, he left the corner to operate from his other tire stores.)

As soon as Oklahoma voted to declare itself "wet," prospective liquor store owners began spying to accuse each other of conspiring to break the law. As soon as Byron Gambulos was granted a license, other licensees in Oklahoma City ganged up in a sort of unofficial and unorganized mafia. Oh! How well I could relate to Byron, because while he was dealing with the liquor mafia of Oklahoma City, I was also dealing with a mafia in the same city—that of the funeral directors and cemetery owners.

Opening Oklahoma to liquor, created great times here. According to tax reports in the mid-60s, Byron's sold at least one third of all liquor purchased in central Oklahoma. The mafia guys tried to buy him out. One of their men even came to see Byron with a suitcase full of money, but no luck. Then his store was bombed—three times. When he was asked who did it, Byron kept his own counsel.

A few days later, carpenters were spotted on the store roof. After that, groups of reporters stood watch day and night, reporting every little movement by the carpenters. When a small cupola began to take shape, it was referred to as "The Crow's Nest." Every night, a man with a federally registered machine gun stood watch for mafia bombers. This weapon, belonging to Byron, was made in Australia during World War II. I remember reading about it in the newspapers as the publicity grew to nationwide. After a while, the state made him take his crow's nest down. The brouhaha slowly died.

BYRON'S LIQUOR WAREHOUSE TODAY

Today, fifty years after the infamous Crow's Nest disappeared, its creator is still living. Retired but still the owner, Byron is, like me, old and gray. I visit his store more than he does, and an entirely new generation works there.

To me, wine specialist and beer aficionado Jason McCormick is the official face of Byron's today. Jason's knowledge of wine and beer is phenomenal, and we have been friends for five years. Just think, when I came to Oklahoma in 1960, he wasn't even born! Does that make him too young—or me too old? There are others at the store who outrank him, but Jason's presence on the floor makes him so visible! He purchased my first book, *Monk to Bootlegger,* and said it was the best book he had ever read. Jason loved the last chapter best, the chapter on liquors. Though I am not modest, I raised an eyebrow at that. Not surprising since Jason is a man absorbed by liquors all day. (Dan Noreen, take notice. I know you are a better writer than I am.)

Jason gets enthralled every time we see each other at Byron's. He is ecstatic when I bring him a wine or beer that he has never seen or tasted. So he always asks me, "Where and how did you get this?" Sometimes I play little games with his mind and let him wonder. Little does he know that I buy these potables online from a Catholic religious goods catalog! After all, did you ever see a Catholic who doesn't drink? The minute I leave, he picks up his phone, and calls Eli Gynther of Oklahoma Beer Imports, presumably asking Eli to see what he can do to import these beverages into the United States and into Oklahoma. Eli has much experience in these imports with a religious overtone. His company imports and distributes Dieu du Ciel beers from French Canada. Eli gets exasperated with me and says he regrets the tone of my emails. (I simply get away with my vibes.)

704

COBRA

*The Indian cobra, Naja naja, shown here with its hood expanded,
is often regarded as the archetypal cobra.*

C obra is Portuguese for "snake." The name is short for cobra de capelo, which means "snake with a hood." Today, most everyone in the world calls it simply cobra.

With the disappearance of Bayou Bob, and the appearance of my old age, I have stopped bottling Viperine, and I play the snake market only on the computer. I peruse the Far East websites searching the cobra dealers. Even at my age, I am still green behind the ears when it comes to oriental trading, and I was rick-a-dooed by several vendors. I now have six cobra rice wine bottles and I'm drawing the line there. I'll sit in my rocking chair and admire them, till thy Kingdom comes.

All over the world, Europe, Africa, Russia and many islands, people have been using viper brandy as a home remedy, except Ireland. It is said that St. Patrick rid the entire Island of snakes when he landed there; he had departed from the still very active Lerins Abbey in the south of France to sail for Eire.

Now that I am old and gray, with nothing else to do, I have turned my interests to cobra rice wine in various countries in the Far East. As a rule, people in Asia hunt cobras, and among other things, will place the live cobra in an empty bottle, fill it up with rice wine, and let the cobra die. Then they will cap it, and everyone in the Orient recognizes it as a home remedy. But beware, there's no licensing in many countries; producers hide in the back of the house, and their wine is of doubtful provenance. When it is done under the counter or in back alleys, beware! Some have died or been left paralyzed by the ingestion of cobra wine made by Gee and by Gosh. Buy only from clean, reputable dealers whom you know to be honest.

From as far away as Thailand, Laos, and Vietnam, I have recently bought cobra rice wine. A nice bottle will normally sell for 300 USD, not cheap but better than taking a trip to the Far East. Personally, I do not use it as a remedy—I am not that crazy. It sits on a shelf in my house, for all my friends to see. Oh, I am proud of it! I am so proud, I've bought others of various sizes, and often at home I play "Now you see it, now you don't" with the original bottle on the shelf of my entryway. What fun I have with my friends!

This bottle is about the size of a fifth of whiskey. The picture to the right was taken on my bed when I woke up one morning. Notice the blinds on the left. I love to sleep and cuddle up with this bottle. I feel just as safe with it, as if I had a good guard dog. If you tell me I've lost my marbles, you're in for a good argument.

The next bottle, below, is from Viet Nam, copied from a Hennessy Cognac bottle in France. If you know Hennessy Cognac as well as I do, you would notice some grapes embossed in the glass on the right side. This cobra has a poisonous scorpion in its mouth. Drinking from this bottle will cure your ailment twice as fast as a bottle that doesn't have the scorpion. This bottle is only seven inches high and you can see the scorpion clearly. Notice the preservative herb in the bottle; Ginseng root adds more potency and a better taste to the wine.

I've never been able to tell the sex of these cobras as I have been able to tell with my French vipers (see *Monk to Bootlegger*). I have long concluded that only French vipers have balls, but I need to go back to college for more education.

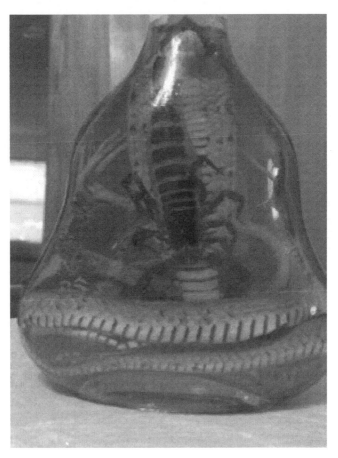

Copy of Hennessy bottle

COBRA RICE WINE

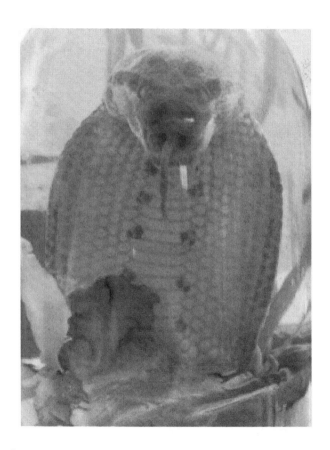

Rice wine, of course, is made by fermenting rice grains and is normally a clear beverage. Sake is a good example. It is found mostly in the Orient where it is more popular than Western drinks. The fermentation process may be manipulated to create a resemblance to Western wine or beer.

A Korean rice wine

There are so many types of rice wine, you could spend a lifetime cataloging them, and there would still be some left. There are as many types as there are enterprising individuals willing to experiment.

My mentor in the study of rice wine was David Spaid of California, the granddaddy of all liquor bottle collectors, who is now very ancient. David published the now-defunct *Miniature Bottle Collector (MBC) Magazine*, and the *Pictorial Bottle Review*. When he felt I was knowledgeable enough to qualify for a degree in herpetology, he gave me, absolutely free of charge, four bottles of cobra rice wine for my collection.

David, you are now old and gray like me, with nothing else to do but wait with good philanthropic thoughts for the Grim Reaper. You are denuding yourself of all worldly accoutrements in order to meet thy Maker.

You are blessed, indeed!

CHAPTER 8

MEDICAL

DR. CRAWFORD

Photo by Michelle

D r. Crawford belongs to the VIP Doctors, and is rated as one of the very best in the State of Oklahoma. He limited his practice to less than 500 patients, whereas he previously had well over 2,000. He guarantees the calls from his patients will be answered within twenty-four hours, day, night, or weekend. Of course you will say that is impossible. But in the office across the hall is fellow VIP Doctor Deck, and the two cover for each other. Dr. Deck also has very good ratings, and my friends LeRoy and Marlene see him even more often than I see Dr. Crawford. It's a good feeling to know we all have the best and most immediate medical service money can buy.

Crawford has been my Docteur for over twenty years, and I've never dreamt of seeing another Docteur. He is lucky to have his wife, Carolyn, an RN, working with him. What an efficient office they have! Carolyn screens all phone calls and patients, and observes the protocol to a tee. For example, one time I called in complaining of cramps in my legs, thinking I would have to be hospitalized. Without any soupçon of rigoletting, she told me, "Joe, simply try to turn all your toes towards your head; and you won't need any medication." Following her advice brought immediate relief from my excruciating pain—and saved me from making an appointment to see Dr. Crawford.

Dr. Crawford is quite a contrast with my previous Docteur. My previous Docteur had lots of trouble understanding my French accent. I had time to die several times while waiting two weeks to see him, and rarely did I talk to his nurse. When I see Carolyn, she goes out of her way to talk to me, and makes sure I understand everything Docteur Crawford tells me.

In 2008, I went into a deep depression. I could not even drive. Docteur Crawford didn't switch me over to a specialist, he stuck by me. Louis, my French friend, drove me several times to see my Docteur, and they both tried to give me mental support, to no avail. Louis brought me food every day for two weeks because I was not eating, getting out of bed, or even looking outdoors: my blinds were all closed.

On a certain Wednesday, I felt lower than ever, just wishing to die. I was lying in my dark and dreary bedroom when Louie came in with lunch. He looked around, placed my lunch on my belly, and took the bull by the horns.

"Joe, let the sun shine in!" He sprinted through the house, opening all the blinds. Though I had to squint at the sun, that was the turning point of my depression. The following Monday, Louie drove me to Docteur Crawford. Doc changed my medicine and encouraged me as far as possible. But I was out of the woods.

Two months later, when I went back to see le Docteur, he looked deeply at me, and with a kind smile, said "Joe, I thought you were a goner."

One year, I had gained weight. Dr. Crawford told me, "Joe, you are twenty pounds over your ideal weight." I acknowledged that my weight often seemed to yo-yo, and I felt helpless to control it. I asked him if he recommended a plan or club to help me out.

"You don't need to join anything, or spend any money. It just takes willpower. You are a courageous man, and you have plenty of willpower when you want to exercise it."

"I used to, Doc, but no more since I had that depression two years ago."

"Darn it, Joe, you don't catch on! Get out of your rut, and simply keep your mouth shut before—and while—you eat."

I hate to write this in this book, but later I complained to Dr. Crawford that I was passing a lot of air, and asked if he might have a pill to eliminate this condition. "Sure, Joe! I'll have some for you as you check out at the window, but don't you know? That's why everybody calls old men old farts."

In closing this essay, I address myself to Docteur Crawford, and indirectly to his wife, Nurse Crawford:

"When I was younger, in the cemetery business, we used to bury your mistakes."

DR. ROYTMAN

Dr. and Mrs. Roytman

While my dermatologist, Dr. Roytman, works on my face, trying to make me look prettier, he regales me with stories of his early days. It seems he was born near the Ukraine in the late 1930s. As he grew up, the situation in the Soviet Union was such that two or three unrelated families might occupy a three-bedroom apartment, sharing a kitchen. A young married couple typically settled into an apartment with their in-laws. Citizens who had worked hard all day, might stand in line for hours just to get food. Just to get a telephone, the wait might be several years!

As a youth Roytman listened to the *Voice of America* radio program and read American classics such as *Tom Sawyer*. Though his father wanted him to become an engineer—and Russian children were expected to obey their parents—Roytman dreamed of a medical career. Surprisingly, Soviet doctors were not held in high regard at the time, earning salaries less than that of a factory worker. However, eventually his father relented, and Roytman began taking night classes to become a doctor, while working days in a cannery.

Roytman completed his education in Italy, where he met his wife. Both Ukrainian Jews, they started off with a lot in common. After completing medical school in 1970, Roytman served as commander of a medical services regiment in the Soviet Union, then began working in a hospital chosen by the government.

Nine years later he came to the conclusion that to better himself professionally, he needed to practice medicine in the United States. "I just didn't see a future there," he said. "I had a desire to grow as a doctor. I wanted to improve myself." The decision to immigrate was not popular at that time. Friends afraid of government pressure shunned him, and he was fired from his hospital job. Finally, seven months later, Roytman, his wife, his small son, and his parents were granted permission to leave the country.

"America offers freedom—freedom to do anything you want," says Roytman. "There are opportunities here for anyone who wants to work. It is just the best country there is."

When Royt questions me about my own youth, instead of entertaining him with my stories, now that I have published *Monk to Bootlegger*, I simply tell him, "Read my book!"

One day while I was flat on the table, and during the ample time in which Dr. Roytman was freezing sunspots on my face, we began discussing the imbibing of spirits.

He asked, "Joe, do you drink?"

"Yes, but I drink responsibly."

"What do you like best?"

"Even though I am a Cognac connoisseur, I prefer beer. How about you, skin Docteur?"

"I love beer also. But it's the first time you called me skin doctor!"

"You always pick at my face!"

"That's to make you pretty, and I love beer also."

"What type of beer and what brand do you prefer?"

"It's a French beer!"

"I know all the French beers, and I am not impressed by them. I prefer the German and darker beers, especially the Belgian Monastic beers. As a former monk, I considered going back to the monastery to drink the beer, but their screening process is too rigorous. Anyway, the darker beers are tastier than the dishwater they pass on as beer. C'mon, tell me your brand!"

"I haven't been able to find it in a while, and I can't remember the name, but it used to be made in Strasbourg."

"Is it La Strassbourgeoise?"

"No, it's got a German name."

"There are no other beers made in Strasbourg. Your mind is slipping!"

"No, I know the beer well. It was made in Strasbourg when the Germans owned it, and the name of the city was different."

I went home, thinking the ole skin doktor was losing his mind. I went to dictionaries—no luck. So I went on the web, and learned that Strasbourg is the name of the French city since World War II, but before that, when the Germans were in possession, it was called Kronembourg.

I ran to the liquor store, and sure enough, they had Kronembourg beer. I purchased a six-pack and took it straight to Dr. Roytman's office.

"I've got to see the Ukrainian! I have something he needs to know!"

"You have no appointment!" the receptionist said, so I dutifully took a seat in the reception room.

When I was let in, Doktor asked, "What brings you in? And what's in your bag?"

When I pulled out the six-pack of Kronembourg, he lit up like a Christmas tree.

"Now you got it! It's the right beer!"

I've been bringing Docteur Roytman a six-pack of Kronembourg every time I have an appointment, and he has never turned it down.

On one visit, I asked Dr. Roytman, "Should I use a soft washcloth to wash my face, or a rough one?" His answer surprised me.

"No cloth at all, and no soap. Simply splash cold water on your face as the Arabs do, it will be better for your skin."

His mention of "like the Arabs" surprised me even more than his recommendation. He sure was to the point, and it showed me he had no prejudice whatsoever. Later, I learned he was a good friend of Docteur Hassoun, my Kuwaiti-born urologist.

Two weeks before Christmas 2014, I gave a signed copy of my book to Docteur Roytman. He thanked me with all types of exclamations, and almost kissed me. Then two days after Christmas, he called me. When I saw his name on my phone ID, I answered in French. On the other end of the phone, I heard laughter, then Docktor said, "Come on, Yosef, don't pull your Frenchie stuff on me. I sent you a nice Christmas card for Christmas, but it was returned due to a wrong address."

"You, a Jew, sent me a Christmas card? That's mighty nice of you! Don't worry about resending the card. I'd rather hear it viva voce direct from you."

"Now you are pulling some Latin on me. Say, I love your book, and I'm learning all about the Catholic church and monks from your writings. I read a little bit every night, and my wife reads it in the daytime."

"When I'm at your office Monday, I'll look into this wrong address business. That could be my fault—after all, I'm a hundred years old."

"Ha! I know you too well. Don't kid me!"

"I am very impressed you thought so well of me as to send me a Christmas card. I hope you and Mrs. Roytman had a nice Hanukkah. See you next week!" Click.

Next time I go see Docteur Roytman, I'll bring him two six-packs of Kronembourg.

DR. HASSOUN

Dr. and Mrs. Hassoun. Photo by Elizabeth.

One Saturday evening I was hurting with what turned out to be a combination bladder and kidney infection. The medical clinic around the corner sent me home with a prescription for antibiotics and an entreaty to see my urologist the following week.

Dr. Hassoun, a native of Kuwait, squeezed me into his calendar at 4:15 p.m., rather late considering the wait time in some doctors' offices lengthens as the day goes on.

Four ladies work in Dr. Hassoun's office. They are receptionist Elizabeth, two assistants, and a nurse.

In addition, the doctor's wife is the bookkeeper, and I always look forward to talking with her. Suzanne Hassoun is from Syria, which was made a French protectorate after World War I. Its educational system is based on the French language and Arabian languages, so most educated Syrians speak French. Speaking French with Suzanne lets me practice the language of my ancestors, while adding a few Muslim words to my vocabulary.

I had to learn the protocol of Muslims as it applies to the Docteur's office. Suzanne is my kind of girl: personable, knowledgeable, and nice-looking. I cannot see or talk to Suzanne anytime I wish. And I cannot write more, lest Docteur Hassoun cut off my pee-wee under the pretext of needed surgery.

Their workday usually ends at the traditional five o'clock, but that day at six, I was the next-to-last patient in the waiting room. The medical part of my visit went fast, but I was hoping the social element would last a while longer.

When I emerged from the examination room at 6:30 p.m., I found bookkeeper Suzanne had already gone home (darn it) to prepare supper for her husband. The other ladies would get home very late and their supper would be cold, yet receptionist Elizabeth still had the perfect smiling mien, and the nurse maintained her usual blank expression. However, the doctor's assistant I passed in the hallway, grimaced at having to go home late—that apparently being my fault!

Hell! How could it have been my fault? My appointment time had been set by the office ladies, and visiting time varies with each patient. If they run more than two hours late, why blame me for it?

Her grimace really bugged me: I was peed off, so the next time I saw her, I also grimaced and stuck my tongue at her—meaning, I hate you little girl, don't play in my yard anymore. She apparently absorbed the message, and since then, every time I see her, we laugh together.

• • •

When I started writing *Monk to Bootlegger*, I often brought a viper brandy to each appointment with Dr. Hassoun. Since we would discuss the sex of snakes, when I brought a French viper, Hassoun pointed out the balls. When I brought my second French viper, he identified it as female and showed me the female organs. I was happy to have such an authority helping me out. However, when I brought in Bayou Bob's rattlesnakes and copperheads to the doctor, search as we might, we never could find the sex organs. We conjectured that only French vipers had balls.

One day at home, I was bottling some brandy which was to include a viper from Bayou Bob. I had placed the live rattlesnake in my kitchen sink, hooding its head so it would not see me manipulating its body, so I could examine the area where its organs should be. Oh! Pressing the belly of a live rattlesnake is an exhilarating feeling! I thought feeling the right spot would produce the sexual organs. Apparently, snakes don't get turned on by humans manipulating their bodies!

Hooded or not, the vipers are not dumb. They are receptive only to the real McCoy.

• • •

Dr. Hassoun has an ample waiting room with lots of magazines, and a Qur'an written in English on the corner table. There's often a wait, hence the magazines. The longer waits give me an opportunity to become a citizen of the world, and catch up with what goes on around the globe. About the time I get absorbed in a story, the assistant opens the inner sanctum door to say, "You are next to see Dr. Hassoun—but first, give us a sample." I'm not concerned about the sample, but what about my magazine story? Perturbed, I swipe the magazine, and place it in my *saccoche*.

• • •

One day in the waiting room, looking for a good magazine, I noticed there was no Qur'an on the table. In its place was a Christian Bible.

How strange! I was mystified! Now, what's happened with Hassoun? Is he giving in? Is Suzanne aware? Does she even know? I simply can't believe it.

Finally, I was called to the examination room. After waiting another half hour, I was really worked up!

Docteur Hassoun, smiling as ever, walked in, meeting my frown. "What's wrong, Joe?"

I could restrain myself no longer. Before he could close the door, I started in on him. "Shame on you, Dr. Hassoun! You don't have the courage of your convictions. I feel sorry for you!"

Hassoun shook his head, interrupted my rant. "I never took the Qur'an out. It simply disappeared. I cannot go one month without a Qur'an missing!"

"What do you think happens?"

"It's obvious, patients take them away."

"Do you think they are Christians who would rather see a Bible there?"

"It's possible, because I didn't place that Bible there." With that statement, Docteur Hassoun disappeared.

A moment later, he reappeared with a Qur'an in his hands. "Since you are concerned about the Qur'an, this one is for you, if you promise me you will read it."

INTER-STIM THERAPY

Dr. Hassoun, MD, Urologist

Bladder problems had been plaguing me for years. Two different urologists had given me various medications, to no avail. After reading a good story on Dr. Hassoun and Dr. Joseph Parkhurst, MD, in WebMD Magazine, I called Dr. Hassoun's office for an appointment.

Though Dr. Hassoun is a Kuwaiti, he speaks English without a trace of Arabic accent. His pleasant personality made me feel at home immediately. After reviewing my list of medications, he declared that I had another option—Bladder Control Therapy (sacral neurostimulation) delivered by the InterStim© System.

After reading more literature, I agreed to have the implant. Similar to a pacemaker, it stimulates the bladder. I went to the hospital as an outpatient, and it took Dr. Hassoun about an hour to implant the device. It had two small wires that he attached to the tail bone (the sacral bone). After a few hours recuperation, I was home by late afternoon.

Now, five years later, the system continues to work well for me.

OLD AND GRAY

"Show me, LORD, my life's end and the number of my days;
let me know how fleeting my life is."

– Psalms 39:4

Now that I am old and gray,
with nothing else to do,
what shall I do?
Monk to Bootlegger is up and about,
what shall I do?

All my friends are old and gray,
With nothing else to do
What shall I do?
My mind is exhausted
with nothing else to do

I prefer to sit in my rocking chair
my beard growing and so is my crop of hair
I shall await the grim reaper
in the person of my Lord
and my God

Yet, what shall I do
if someone new the morning brings?
How will I comb over the gray
and hide this chair behind me?
Who shall I thank
as I invite her in?

ABOUT JOSEPH JERRY LEVESQUE

Born 1927 in Maine, Joseph spoke only French until age 17. After two years in the Navy, he returned home and became a snowshoe racing champion in Maine. The mayor of Montreal awarded Joseph the key to the city after he walked 300 miles on snowshoes to attend an international snowshoe convention.

After becoming a Catholic monk, Joseph founded not only the Brothers of St. Joseph in Oklahoma City, but also Resurrection Cemetery which boasts the most unique cemetery chapel in North America. A world traveler, he published *The Cognac Newsletter* for collectors, and authored numerous articles for various publications.

Later he bootlegged bottles from Andorra and France to the United States, and was the only American producer of clandestine Viper Brandy for decades.

Photo by Carolyn Crawford RN, OKC

Joseph has always been unconventional. He discusses his Viper Brandy with his doctor; brings beer to his dermatologist; and explores the sex of snakes with his urologist.

Finis

Made in the USA
Charleston, SC
10 April 2016